My Daily Psalm Book

The Book of Psalms Arranged for Each Day of the Week

Msgr. Austin P. Bennett, JCD, P.A.

NIHIL OBSTAT:

GEORGIUS A. DENZER, S.T.D.
Censor Deputatus

IMPRIMATUR:

THOMAS EDMUNDUS MOLLOY, S. T. D.
Episcopus Brooklyniensis.

Brooklyni, XII Augusti 1947.

Copyright 1947 by Confraternity of the Precious Blood
Printed in India

All Rights Reserved Under International Copyright Convention
All Rights Reserved Under Pan-American Copyright Convention

We are privileged to present below a letter from the Rev. Augustine Bea, S.J., Rector of the Pontifical Biblical Institute.

In the new Latin translation of the Psalms which our Holy Father, Pope Pius XII, had ordered to be made and then subsequently approved, He has given not only to priests, but to all the faithful a powerful incentive to use these inspired hymns and prayers with frequency and devotion. The Vicar of Christ points especially to the rich fruits which come from the reading of the Psalms: they hold up shining examples of sanctity before our eyes, nourish within us the love of God and increase sentiments of Christian fortitude and the spirit of true contrition. In a word. they give us light, grace and comfort. We should hold it a singular grace that, in these difficult times, the Holy Father has referred us to this sacred book, for out of it we may draw, as did the people of Israel in days of past tribulations (I Mach. 12:9), strength and consolation in our needs of the present. May the Psalms bring abundant blessings to all those who pray and read them with devotion!

Rome, May 25, 1947
Feast of Pentecost.

AUGUSTINUS BEA S.J.
Rector of the Pontifical Biblical Institute.

FOREWORD

The Perfect Prayer Book for Everyone

IN presenting this pocket-edition of the Book of Psalms, we are placing within the reach of everyone a book of perfect prayer.

The psalms are prayers in which God Himself teaches us how to pray; for they were written under the direct inspiration of the Holy Spirit. Herein we have the answer to the question: "What prayers shall I say?" Why the prayers of Holy Scripture itself! "There is no need to scrape together endless man-made prayers when Sacred Scripture frames the very thoughts of God." The psalms are the vital presentation of God's inspirations and man's aspirations; they are the ideal manifestations of man's hunger and thirst after God and of God's loving response to man. Of great age, they are ever new and appropriate. They are as satisfying and stimulating to us of the twentieth century as they were to men before the birth of Christ and down through the Apostolic and Middle Ages.

The Holy Father and the Psalms

IN His Apostolic Letter authorizing the new translation of the Psalms, The Vicar of Christ writes: "Following the example of her Divine Redeemer and His Apostles, the Church, from her earliest beginnings, has made constant use of these illustrious songs, which the holy prophet David and other sacred writers composed under the inspiration of the Divine Spirit. They occupy a place apart in the official prayer that priests recite each day in praise of God's goodness and majesty, for their own needs, and for those of the universal Church and of the entire world."

The Universal Manual

THIS book of Psalms is for all times, all circumstances and all needs. It is for everybody. The psalms rhyme with every mood of man. No longing of the soul, no craving of the mind, no bodily want exists which cannot be expressed in the sublime phrases of the psalms. Prayers in the morning, during the day, for guidance in work, of repentance for sin, of thanksgiving, of adoration, prayers for loved ones and for all the world, prayers in the evening, prayers in time of trouble or sickness and countless others are to be found in this Book of Psalms. This perfect Prayer Book was the book of praise and prayer used by the ancient Jews in the worship of the Temple and in that of the home. It was the prayer book of Our Lord and Our Lady, of the Apostles and the first Christians, of all the Popes from St. Peter to Pius XII, of all the Blessed from St. Stephen to Mother Cabrini, of the clergy and the laity of the ages.

Praying With the Church

THE arrangement of the psalms according to the days of the week follows that of the official prayer book of the Church, the Breviary. The Clergy and Religious recite these very prayers daily. The psalms form the greater part of the Divine Office which Holy Mother Church offers, day and night throughout the world, to the end of time. This echo of the worship of the heavenly choirs is offered for the honor and glory of God and the salvation of the world. Only the Mass is of greater dignity and worth; only the Missal can surpass the Book of Psalms in dignity and scope. And the Missal draws heavily upon the Psalter.

The Missal and the Psalms

THE Holy Sacrifice of the Mass enshrines many quotations from the Book of Psalms. Hence the Sacrifice of the Mass and the Sacrifice of Praise, which is the Divine Office, are closely allied, so that the Missal and the Psalm Book are companion-volumes. As members of Holy Mother Church, all Catholics share in the privilege and duty of adoring God through Christ. Let us then offer our praises and prayers to God in the spirit of Holy Mother Church and in active union with her perfect worship by making use of that divinely-inspired volume which she has been using for two thousand years, the Book of Psalms. Praying the psalms unites us with the unending and perfect praise and prayer of heaven and earth. The Psalter is truly the primary and best Catholic prayer book.

Illustrations

THE illustrations found in this book are all original and especially designed with key phrases to furnish a pictorial guide to the spirit and meaning of the psalms. They are the work of the noted artist, Ariel Agemian, who has labored untiringly during the past three years to achieve this extraordinary work. It is interesting to note that this is the first time that the entire Psalter has been illustrated.

Priests and Religious—The New Psalter

PRIESTS and religious will find this book, which is a translation of the New Psalter, a great help in the recitation of the Divine Office. The new version has greatly clarified many of the obscure passages of the old version. We feel confident it will fill a great need and help tremendously toward a better appreciation of the Breviary and its devout recitation. It should prove a very helpful companion-volume to the Breviary.

How to Pray the Psalms

WE must make these psalms the expression of our own personal prayer-life. In the enemies of which David speaks so frequently, we can see our own spiritual enemies, satan, sin and temptation. The deep love for Jerusalem expressed by the psalmist we can take over and apply to the Church, to Christ Himself. You need not say all the psalms as given for each day. It is well to choose those that fit your present needs and circumstances. On page x you will find a helpful guide in the use of the psalms.

TO His Excellency, Most Rev. Thomas E. Molloy, S.T.D. we are deeply indebted for the gracious encouragement he has afforded us.

To the Rev. John E. Steinmueller, S.T.D., S.Scr.L., Professor of Sacred Scripture at the Seminary of the Immaculate Conception, Huntington, L. I., we are profoundly obligated for his invaluable assistance and scholarly criticism in the preparation of this work.

To Kathryn Sullivan, R.S.C.J., Ph.D., Professor of Sacred Scripture and History at the College of the Sacred Heart, Manhattanville, N. Y., we extend our sincere appreciation for her painstaking labor in proofreading our manuscripts and for proposing many helpful improvements.

To the Sisters Adorers of the Precious Blood we express our heartfelt thanks for their constant prayerful assistance which has made possible the works of the Confraternity.

(REV.) JOSEPH B. FREY.

Feast of Our Lady
July 16, 1947

PSALM GUIDE

PRAYER GUIDE

Ps. 1—Preface to the Book of Psalms. David contrasts the two paths followed by all men in their search for happiness. Note the fruitful tree and the wind driven chaff: the good and the wicked.

The Two Ways

I Nocturn **PSALM 1** Matins

HAPPY the man who follows not * the counsel of the wicked,

Nor enters upon the path of sinners, * nor sits in the assembly of the insolent;

2. But his delight is in the law of the Lord, * and he meditates on his law day and night.

3. And he is like a tree * planted beside streams of water,

That yields fruit in due season, whose leaves do not wither, * and whatever he does, prospers.

4. Not so the wicked, not so, * but they are like chaff which the wind scatters.

5. Therefore the wicked shall not stand firm in the judgment, * nor sinners in the gathering of the just.

6. For the Lord takes care of the way of the just, * but the course of the wicked shall end in ruin.

The Messianic King

PSALM 2

WHY do the nations rage, * and the peoples plot in vain?

2. The kings of the earth rise up and rulers conspire together * against the Lord and His anointed:

3. "Let us break their bonds * and cast their fetters from us!"

4. He who dwells in heaven laughs, * the Lord mocks them.

5. Then in his anger he speaks to them, * and in his wrath he dismays them.

6. "I, indeed, have set up my king * on Sion, my holy hill!"

7. I will proclaim the decree of the Lord: The Lord said to me: * "Thou art my son, this day have I begotten thee.

Ps. 2—*The first rebel Satan is defeated by the invincible authority of the Messias who is crowned with royal power. An earthly king offers his crown to the Messias in token of his obedience. Usurpers of power are fleeing from divine anger.*

---

8. Ask of me and I will give thee the nations for thy inheritance, * the ends of the earth for thy possession.

9. Thou shalt rule them with an iron rod; * thou shalt shatter them like a potter's vessel."

10. Now then, O kings, be wise; * take warning, O judges of the earth.

11. Serve the Lord in fear, and rejoice in him; * with trembling offer homage to him, Lest he be angry, and you perish, when suddenly his anger is enkindled: * happy are all who take refuge in him.

Ps. 3—*David, having fled his foe, set up his tent for the night. In the morning he thanks God for his protection during the night and bids us trust God in future conflicts . . . A truly sublime morning prayer.*

Morning Prayer

PSALM 3

O LORD how many are my adversaries, * many rise up against me!

3. There are many who say of me: "There is no help for him in God."

4. But thou, O Lord art my shield, * my glory, the one who lifts up my head.

5. With a loud voice I cried unto the Lord, * and he answered me from his holy mountain.

6. I lay down and slept: * I arose for the Lord upholds me.

7. I shall not fear even thousands of people, * arrayed against me on every side.

8. Arise O Lord! * Save me, my God! For thou hast struck all my enemies on the jaw, * thou hast broken the teeth of the wicked.

9. Salvation is of the Lord: * thy blessing be upon thy people!

The Greatness of God; the God-given Dignity of Man

PSALM 8

II Nocturn

O LORD, our Lord, how wonderful is thy name in all the earth, * thou who hast proclaimed thy glory upon the heavens.

3. Out of the mouths of infants and babes thou hast prepared praise to confuse thy adversaries, * to silence the enemy and the revengeful.

4. When I gaze at thy heavens, the work of thy fingers, * the moon and the stars which thou hast made:

5. What is man, that thou art mindful of him? * or the son of man, that thou dost take care of him?

Ps. 8—*The Psalmist marvels at God's glory in the heavens and His goodness to man who though less than the angel is above every other creature. Note angel, man, animal and plant life, stars and seas.*

---

6. Thou hast made him a little less than the angels, * with glory and honor thou hast crowned him;

7. Thou hast given him power over the works of thy hands, * thou hast put all things under his feet:

8. Sheep and oxen, all of them, * and also the beasts of the field.

9. The birds of the air and the fish of the sea: * whatever moves along the paths of the seas.

10. O Lord, our Lord, * how wonderful is thy name in all the earth!

Thanksgiving for Victory

PSALM 9A, I

I WILL thank thee, O Lord, with all my heart, * I will tell of all thy wondrous deeds.

3. I will be glad and rejoice in thee, * I will sing praise to thy name, O Most High,

4. Because my enemies have retreated, * they are overthrown and have perished before thee.

5. For thou hast taken up my just cause, * thou hast taken thy seat upon the throne as a just judge.

6. Thou hast rebuked the nations, destroyed the wicked, * thou hast blotted out their name forever.

7. The foes are vanquished, ruined forever, * thou hast destroyed their cities: the memory of them has vanished.

8. But the Lord sits enthroned forever, * he has set up his throne for judgment.

9. And he himself will judge the world with justice, * pass sentence on the nations with equity.

10. And the Lord will be a refuge for the oppressed, * a ready refuge in times of trouble.

11. They who know thy name will trust in thee, * for thou dost not abandon those who seek thee, O Lord.

Ps. 9A, ii—Besieged in the fortress of Sion David and his people pray for deliverance from the approaching army and for protection against the enemy.

Praise God; He is a Just Avenger

PSALM 9A, II

SING praises to the Lord who dwells in Sion, * publish his works among the peoples,

13. For as an avenger of blood he has remembered them, * he has not forgotten the cry of the poor.

14. Have pity on me, O Lord, behold the affliction which I suffer from my enemies, * thou who dost raise me up from the gates of death,

15. That I may proclaim all thy praises in the gates of the daughter of Sion, * and rejoice because of thy help.

16. The nations have sunk into the pit which they dug, * their foot is caught in the net which they hid.

17. The Lord has revealed himself, he has executed judgment; * the sinner is trapped in the works of his own hands.

18. Let sinners descend into hell, * all nations that forget God.

19. For the needy shall not always be forgotten, * nor shall the hope of the poor perish forever.

20. Arise, O Lord: let not man prevail: * let the nations be judged in thy presence.

21. Strike them with terror, O Lord; * let the nations know that they are but men.

An Appeal to God Against the Wicked

PSALM 9B, III

III Nocturn

WHY, O Lord, dost thou stand afar off, * and hide thyself in times of trouble,

2. While the wicked man is puffed up, the needy man is distressed, * the latter is trapped in the plots the former has devised.

3. For the sinner boasts of his greed, and the robber curses and spurns the Lord.

4. In a spirit of pride the wicked one says: "He will not seek vengeance; * there is no God:" Such is the sum of all his thoughts.
5. Prosperous are his ways at all times; thy judgments are farthest from his mind; * he despises all his enemies.
6. He says to himself "I shall not waver; * throughout the ages I shall not be unhappy."
7. His mouth is full of cursing, deceit and violence, * under his tongue are trouble and mischief.
8. He waits in ambush near the villages, in hiding places he murders the innocent; * his eyes spy upon the poor man.
9. He lurks in secret places like a lion in nis lair; he lies in ambush to catch the poor: * he seizes the poor and drags him into his net.
10. He crouches, he crawls on the ground, * and the helpless fall before his violence.
11. He says to himself: "God has forgotten, * he has turned away his face, he never sees."

Blunder to Slight God or His Poor

PSALM 9B, IV

ARISE, Lord God, lift up thy hand! * forget not the poor!
13. Why does the wicked despise God, * and say to himself: "He will not seek vengeance?"

Ps. 9B, iv—The Lord is "the helper of the orphan."

14. But thou dost see: thou lookest upon trouble and pain, * that thou mayest take them into thy care.

To thee the poor man entrusts himself, * thou art the helper of the orphan!

15. Break thou the arm of the sinner and the evil-doer: * avenge his wickedness, so that no trace of it remains.

16. The Lord is king forever and ever, * the nations have perished from his land.

17. Thou, O Lord, hast heard the desire of the humble, * thou hast strengthened their heart and listened to them,

18. So as to safeguard the right of the orphan and oppressed, * and that mere man may no longer cause terror.

Prayer for Confidence

PSALM 10

IN the Lord I take refuge; how can you say to me: * "Fly away like a bird to the mountain!

2. For, see the wicked bend the bow, they fit their arrow to the string, * to shoot in the dark at the upright of heart.

3. When the foundations are overthrown, * what can the just man do?"

4. The Lord is in his holy temple; * the Lord's throne is in heaven.

His eyes see, * his glances test the children of men.

5. The Lord tries the just and the wicked; * he hates the lover of evil.

6. He will pour down burning coals and brimstone upon the wicked; * the scorching wind shall be the portion of their cup.

7. For the Lord is just, he loves justice; * the upright shall behold his face.

The Almighty Lord of the World

PSALM 92

Lauds

THE Lord is king, he is robed in majesty, * the Lord is clothed with power, he has girded himself,

Ps. 92—*Mightier than the surgings of the sea is the Lord, King of all creation.*

And has established the world, * which will never totter.

2. Thy throne stands firm from the beginning, * thou art from eternity.

3. The floods rise, O Lord, the floods lift up their voice, * the floods lift up their roar.

4. Mightier than the sound of many waters, mightier than the surgings of the sea: * mighty is the Lord on high.

5. Exceedingly trustworthy are thy testimonies; * holiness befits thy house, O Lord, forevermore.

Ps. 99—Priests invite people to enter the temple to proclaim the goodness and mercy of God, their Creator and Shepherd.

Call to Worshippers Entering Temple

PSALM 99

ACCLAIM the Lord, all the earth; * serve the Lord with gladness.

Go into his presence * with great joy.

3. Know that the Lord is God: he made us and we are his, * his people and the sheep of his pasture.

4. Enter his gates with praise, his courts with a hymn; * give thanks to him, bless his name.

5. For the Lord is good, his mercy is forever, * and his faithfulness is for ages unending.

Ps. 62—The great fervor and devotion of a soul united with God. Isolated from the visible world, he holds and presses to his heart the Infinite—the possession of God.

Prayer Before Holy Communion

PSALM 62

O GOD, thou art my God: * earnestly I seek thee,

My soul thirsts for thee, my flesh longs for thee * like a dry and parched land without water.

3. So I look for thee in the sanctuary, * to see thy power and thy glory.

4. Because thy kindness is better than life, * my lips shall praise thee.

5. So will I bless thee all my life, * in thy name I will lift up my hands.

6. As with marrow and fat my soul is satiated, * and my mouth praises thee with joyful lips,

7. When I remember thee on my couch, * and meditate on thee in the night watches.

8. For thou art my helper, * and I rejoice in the shadow of thy wings.

9. My soul clings close to thee, * thy right hand upholds me.

10. But they who seek to take my life, * shall go into the depths of the earth.

11. They shall be delivered over to the power of the sword, * they shall be the prey of the jackals.

12. But the king shall rejoice in God, everyone who swears by him shall glory, * because the mouth of liars shall be stopped.

Canticle of the Three Young Men

DAN. 3, 57-88

ALL works of the Lord, bless the Lord; * praise and glorify him forever.

58. Angels of the Lord, bless the Lord; *

59. Heavens, bless the Lord,

60. All the waters above the clouds,

61. bless the Lord; * all the hosts of the Lord, bless the Lord.

Three young men, because of their refusal to adore a false god, were cast into a fiery furnace. They are calling all God's creatures to praise Him.

62. Sun and moon, bless the Lord; *
63. stars of heaven, bless the Lord.
64. All showers and dews, bless the Lord; *
65. all winds, bless the Lord.
66. Fire and heat, bless the Lord; *
67. chill and cold, bless the Lord.
68. Dews and rains, bless the Lord; *
69. ice and frost, bless the Lord.
70. Ice and snow, bless the Lord; *
71. nights and days, bless the Lord.
72. Light and darkness, bless the Lord; *
73. lightnings and clouds, bless the Lord.
74. Let the earth bless the Lord; * praise and glorify him forever.
75. Mountains and hills, bless the Lord; *

76. All plants that grow upon the earth, bless the Lord.

77. Fountains, bless the Lord; *

78. Seas and rivers, bless the Lord.

79. Sea-monsters and everything that moves in the waters, bless the Lord; *

80. all birds of the air, bless the Lord.

81. All beasts and cattle, bless the Lord; * praise and glorify him forever.

82. Sons of men, bless the Lord; *

83. let Israel bless the Lord.

84. Priests of the Lord, bless the Lord; *

85. servants of the Lord, bless the Lord.

86. Spirits and souls of the just, bless the

87. Lord; * holy and humble of heart, bless the Lord.

88. Ananias, Azarias and Misael, bless the Lord; * praise Him and glorify Him forever. Let us bless the Father and the Son with the Holy Spirit: * let us praise and glorify him forever.

56. Blessed art thou in the firmament of heaven; * and worthy of praise and glorified forever.

Ps. 148—All men are called upon to praise God: at the dawn of infancy, in the full daylight of youth and in the darkness of old age as pictured in this tryptych.

A Call to All Creatures to Praise God

PSALM 148

ALLELUIA!
Praise the Lord from the heavens, * praise him in the heights.

2. Praise him, all his angels, * praise him all his hosts.

3. Praise him, sun and moon, * praise him all you twinkling stars.

4. Praise him highest heavens, * and waters that are above the heavens.

5. Let them praise the name of the Lord, * for he commanded and they were created.

6. He made them stand firm forever and ever: * he laid down a law which shall not be revoked.
7. Praise the Lord from the earth, * sea monsters and all depths of the sea.
8. Fire, hail, snow and fog, * stormy winds, that do his bidding.
9. Mountains and all hills, * fruit trees and all cedars.
10. Wild beasts and all cattle, * reptiles, and winged birds.
11. Kings of the earth and all peoples, * princes and all judges of the earth.
12. Young men and virgins too, * old men together with children:
13. Let them praise the name of the Lord, * for his name alone is sublime.
14. His glory is above heaven and earth, * and he has given great strength to his people.
A theme of praise for all his faithful, * the children of Israel, a people near unto him.

Prayer of Thanksgiving

PSALM 117

Prime

GIVE thanks to the Lord for he is good; * for his mercy endures forever.
2. Let the house of Israel declare: * "His mercy endures forever."

Ps. 117—A procession of pilgrims carrying palm-branches enters the sacred courts of the temple: it is the Feast of Tabernacles. They chant a song of thanksgiving.

---

3. Let the house of Aaron declare: * "His mercy endures forever."

4. Let those who fear the Lord declare: * "His mercy endures forever."

5. From the depths of distress I called upon the Lord; * the Lord answered me and rescued me.

6. The Lord is with me: I do not fear; * what can man do to me?

7. The Lord is with me, my helper, * and I shall see my enemies put to shame.

8. It is better to take refuge in the Lord, * than to trust in man.

9. It is better to take refuge in the Lord, * than to trust in princes.

10. All the nations surrounded me: * in the name of the Lord I destroyed them.

11. On all sides they surrounded me: in the name of the Lord I destroyed them.

12. They swarmed around me like bees; they blazed like a fire among thorns: * in the name of the Lord I destroyed them.

13. I was pushed violently, so that I might fall; * but the Lord helped me.

14. The Lord is my strength and my courage; * and he has become my savior.

15. A cry of joy and of deliverance * *resounds* in the tents of the just:

16. The right hand of the Lord has done valiantly, the right hand of the Lord has lifted me up, * the right hand of the Lord has done valiantly.

17. I shall not die, but live; * and I shall proclaim the works of the Lord.

18. The Lord has chastised me severely, * but he has not given me over to death.

19. Open to me the gates of justice; * I will pass through them and give thanks to the Lord.

20. This is the gate of the Lord, * the just shall enter through it.

21. I will give thanks to thee for thou hast heard me, * and hast become my savior.

22. The stone, which the builders rejected, * has become the cornerstone.

23. This is the Lord's doing; * it is wonderful in our eyes.

24. This is the day which the Lord has made; * let us rejoice and be glad of it.

25. O, Lord, save; * O, Lord, grant success!

26. Blessed is he who comes in the name of the Lord; we bless you from the house of the Lord. *

27. The Lord is God, and he shows us his light.

Arrange a solemn procession with leafy branches * even to the horns of the altar.

28. Thou art my God, and I give thanks to thee; * my God I exalt thee.

29. Give thanks to God, for he is good, * his mercy endures forever.

The Blessings of the Law

PSALM 118, I

HAPPY are the blameless in life's way, * who walk in the law of the Lord.

2. Happy are they who observe his decrees, * who seek him with their whole heart,

3. Who do no wrong, * but walk in his ways.

Ps. 118, i—A young man venerating the Law of God as a source of happiness and a safeguard against sin.

4. Thou hast given us thy precepts, * to be zealously observed.

5. O that my conduct may be steadfast * in observing thy statutes.

6. Then I shall not be put to shame, * when I have regard for all thy commandments.

7. I will praise thee with a sincere heart, * when I learn thy just ordinances.

8. I will obey thy statutes: * forsake me not utterly.

9. How can a youth lead a pure life? * by heeding thy words.

10. I seek thee with all my heart; * let me not wander from thy commandments.

11. I treasure thy word in my heart, * that I may not sin against thee.

12. Blessed art thou, O Lord; * teach me thy statutes.
13. With my lips I announce * all the ordinances of thy mouth.
14. I rejoice in the way of thy decrees, * as much as in all riches.
15. I will meditate on thy precepts, * I will regard thy ways.
16. I will take pleasure in thy statutes: * I will not forget thy words.

God's Law a Help in Distress

PSALM 118, II

DEAL kindly with thy servant that I may live * and keep thy words.
18. Open my eyes, * that I may behold the wonders of thy law.
19. I am a pilgrim on earth, * hide not thy commandments from me.
20. My soul is consumed * with longing for thy ordinances at all times.
21. Thou hast rebuked the proud; * accursed are they who turn aside from thy commandments.
22. Take away from me reproach and contempt, * because I observe thy decrees.
23. Though princes sit together and talk against me, * thy servant meditates on thy statutes.

*Ps. 118i ii—"I am a pilgrim on earth, * hide not thy commandments from me."*

24. For thy decrees are my delight, * thy statutes, my counsellors.
25. My soul is prostrate in the dust; * revive me according to thy word.
26. I have made known my ways and thou hast answered me: * teach me thy statutes.
27. Make me to understand the way of thy precepts, * that I may meditate on thy wondrous works.
28. My soul sheds tears because of sorrow, * lift me up according to thy word.
29. Keep me from the way of error * and graciously grant me thy law.
30. I have chosen the way of truth, * I have set thy ordinances before me.
31. I cling to thy decrees; * O Lord, put me not to shame.

32. I will run in the way of thy commandments, * when thou dost enlarge my heart.

The Law Helps Us to Avoid Sin

PSALM 118, III

Terce

SHOW me the way of thy statutes, O Lord, * and I will keep it perfectly.

34. Give me understanding that I may observe thy law, * and keep it with my whole heart.

35. Lead me in the path of thy commandments, * for I delight therein.

36. Incline my heart to thy decrees, and not to greed.

37. Turn away my eyes from beholding vanity; * through thy way give me life.

38. Fulfill thy promise to thy servant, * which was given to them who fear thee.

39. Take away my shame which I fear, * for thy ordinances are good.

40. Behold, I long for thy precepts: * vivify me according to thy justice.

41. Let thy mercies come upon me, O Lord, * thy help, according to thy promise.

42. Then shall I answer those who insult me, * for I trust in thy words.

Ps. 118, iii—The Psalmist turns toward the Divine Law on the horizon, which leads him away from vanity and greed to freedom in God.

---

43. Take not the word of truth from my mouth, * for I trust in thy ordinances.

44. So shall I always keep thy law, * for ever and ever.

45. And I will walk on a wide path, * for I seek thy precepts.

46. I will also speak of thy decrees before kings, * and will not be ashamed.

47. I will be delighted with thy commandments, * which I love.

48. I will lift up my hands to thy commandments * and I will meditate on thy statutes.

Ps. 118, iv—At night when he rises to pray, all enveloped in Divine Light, he calls God his portion.

PSALM 118, IV

The Law Affords Consolation

REMEMBER thy word to thy servant, * by which thou hast given me hope.

50. This is my consolation in my affliction, * that thy word revives me.

51. The proud are most insulting to me; * but I depart not from thy law.

52. I remember thy judgments of old, O Lord, * and I am comforted.

53. Indignation seizes me because of the wicked, * who forsake thy law.

54. Thy statutes are the theme of my song * in the place of my pilgrimage.

55. In the night I remember thy name, O Lord, * and I will keep thy law.

56. This happened to me, * because I observed thy precepts.
57. I have said, O Lord, that my portion is * to keep thy words.
58. I seek thy favor with my whole heart, * have mercy on me according to thy promise.
59. I thought over my ways, * and turned my steps toward thy decrees.
60. I made haste and delayed not, * to keep thy commandments.
61. The snares of the wicked surround me: * I have not forgotten thy law.
62. At midnight I rise to thank thee * because of thy just ordinances.
63. I am a companion of all who fear thee * of all that keep thy precepts.
64. The earth, O Lord, is full of thy loving kindness; * teach me thy statutes.

PSALM 118, V

God's Goodness in the Law

THOU hast dealt kindly with thy servant, * O Lord, according to thy word.
66. Teach me good judgment and knowledge, * for I trust in thy commandments.
67. Before I was afflicted, I went astray, * but now I keep thy word.

Ps. 118, v—He thanks God for having humiliated his persecutors and prays that the Divine Hand may enlighten his soul also.

---

68. Thou art good and beneficent; * teach me thy statutes.

69. The proud invent lies against me, * I observe thy precepts with my whole heart.

70. Their heart is as gross as fat; * I delight in thy law.

71. It is good for me that I was afflicted, * that I may learn thy statutes.

72. The law of thy mouth is dearer to me, * than immeasurable gold and silver.

73. Thy hands have made me and fashioned me; * give me understanding, that I may learn thy commandments.

74. They who fear thee, see me and are glad, * for I have hoped in thy word.

75. I know, O Lord, that thy ordinances are right, * and justly hast thou afflicted me.
76. Let thy loving kindness be present to comfort me; * according to the promise thou gavest to thy servant.
77. Let thy tender mercies come unto me, that I may live, * for thy law is my delight.
78. Let the proud be put to shame, for they afflict me unjustly; * I will meditate on thy precepts.
79. Let those who fear thee turn to me, * and those who know thy decrees.
80. Let my heart be perfect in thy statutes, * that I may not be put to shame.

PSALM 118, VI

Sext

The Law is True

MY soul longs for thy help; * in thy word do I hope.
82. My eyes long for thy word: * when wilt thou comfort me?
83. Though I have become like a wineskin in the smoke, * I have not forgotten thy statutes.
84. How many are the days of thy servant? * when wilt thou execute judgment upon my persecutors?
85. The proud dug pits for me, * they who do not act according to thy law.

*Ps. 118, vi—"They almost destroyed me on earth, * but I have not forsaken thy precepts."*

---

86. All thy commandments are true; * they persecute me unjustly: do thou help me.
87. They almost destroyed me on earth, * but I have not forsaken thy precepts.
88. According to thy loving kindness keep me alive, * and I will observe the decrees of thy mouth.
89. Thy word, O Lord, is forever * firm as heaven.
90. Thy faithfulness endures throughout the ages; * thou hast founded the earth and it abides.
91. According to thy ordinances, they remain always, * for all things serve thee.
92. If thy law had not been my delight, * I would have perished in my affliction.
93. Never will I forget thy precepts, * for thereby hast thou kept me alive.
94. I am thine: save me, * for I have studied thy precepts.

95. The wicked lie in wait to destroy me; * but I give heed to thy decrees.

96. I have seen the limit of all human perfection: * thy commandment is limitless.

God's Law Gives Wisdom

PSALM 118, VII

HOW I love thy law, O Lord! * it is my meditation all day long.

98. Thy commandment has made me wiser than my enemies, * for it is ever with me.

99. I am wiser than all my teachers, * for thy decrees are my meditation.

100. I have greater understanding than the aged, * because I observe thy precepts.

101. I withhold my feet from every evil path * that I may observe thy words.

102. I have not swerved from thy ordinances, * for thou hast taught me.

103. How sweet to my palate are thy words! * sweeter than honey to my mouth.

104. Through thy precepts I gain understanding, * therefore, I hate every way of iniquity.

Ps. 118, vii—*He expresses his love for the Lord and in virtue of this love the Divine Law is a lamp to his feet and a light to his path.*

---

105. Thy word is a lamp to my feet, * and a light to my path.

106. I swear and am determined * to keep thy just ordinances.

107. Great is my affliction, O Lord: * revive me according to thy word.

108. Accept O Lord the offerings of my mouth, * and teach me thy ordinances.

109. My life is always in danger, * but I do not forget thy law.

110. Sinners have laid a snare for me, * but I have not strayed from thy precepts.

111. Thy decrees are my heritage forever, * because they are the joy of my heart.

112. I have set my heart to fulfill thy statutes: * perpetually, perfectly.

Loyalty to the Law

PSALM 118, VIII

I HATE half-hearted men, * but I love thy law.
114. Thou art my shelter and my shield: * I hope in thy word.

115. Depart from me, evil-doers, * that I may observe the commandments of my God.

116. Uphold me according to thy promise that I may live; * disappoint me not in my hope.

117. Support me and I shall be safe, * and I will always give heed to thy statutes.

118. Thou despisest all who depart from thy statutes, * for their thought is deceitful.

119. All sinners of earth are as dross to thee, * therefore do I love thy decrees.

120. My flesh shudders for fear of thee, * and I am afraid of thy ordinances.

121. I have done what is right and practised justice: * abandon me not to my oppressors.

122. Be a guarantee for thy servant's welfare, * lest the proud oppress me.

122. Be a guarantee for thy servant's welfare, * lest the proud oppress me.

Ps. 118, viii—*Lightning strikes and destroys the temple: men flee in panic. A picture of God's judgment on sin. "My flesh shudders for fear of thee," the fear to offend God by breaking his commandments.*

---

123. My eyes long for thy salvation, * and for thy just word.

124. Deal with thy servant according to thy goodness, * and teach me thy statutes.

125. I am thy servant, give me understanding, * that I may know thy decrees.

126. It is time for the Lord to act: * they have broken thy law.

127. Therefore I love thy commandments, * more than gold, more than fine gold.

128. Therefore have I chosen for myself all thy precepts; * I hate every form of deceit.

Ps. 118, ix—"The revelation of thy words enlightens . . . deliver me from the oppression of men, and I will keep thy precepts."

God's Law is Marvelous

PSALM 118, IX

None

WONDERFUL are thy decrees, * therefore my soul observes them.

130. The revelation of thy words enlightens, * it makes the simple understand.

131. I open wide my mouth and sigh, * because I long for thy commandments.

132. Turn to me and be gracious to me, * as is thy wont towards those who love thy name.

133. Direct my steps according to thy word, * and let no wickedness dominate me.

134. Deliver me from the oppression of men, * and I will keep thy precepts.

135. Look with favor upon thy servant, * and teach me thy statutes.

136. Streams of tears flow from my eyes, * because men do not keep thy law.

137. Thou art just, O Lord, * and just is thy judgment.

138. With justice thou hast enjoined thy decrees, * and with great firmness.

139. My zeal consumes me, * because my enemies forget thy words.

140. Thy word is exceedingly refined, * and thy servant loves it.

141. Little am I and despised; * yet I forget not thy precepts.

142. Thy justice is justice forever, * and thy law is firm.

143. Distress and anguish have come upon me, * yet thy commandments are my delight.

144. The justice of thy decrees is everlasting, * give me understanding and I shall live.

Ps. 118, x—"I cry with all my heart: hear me, O Lord . . . Near at hand are those who persecute me . . . Look upon my misery and rescue me, for I have not forgotten thy taw. Plead my cause and deliver me."

Fidelity to the Law

PSALM 118, X

I CRY with all my heart: hear me, O Lord; * I keep thy statutes.

146. I cry unto thee, save me; * that I may keep thy decrees.

147. I come at dawn and cry for help; * I trust in thy words.

148. My eyes anticipate the night-watches, * that I may meditate on thy word.

149. In thy great kindness hear my voice, O Lord, * and according to thy judgment revive me.

150. Near at hand are those who persecute me unjustly, * they are far from thy law.

151. Thou art near, O Lord, * and all thy commandments are true.

152. Long ago I knew from thy decrees * that thou hast founded them forever.

153. Look upon my misery and rescue me, * for I have not forgotten thy law.

154. Plead my cause and deliver me; * revive me according to thy word.

155. Salvation is far from sinners, * because they give no heed to thy statutes.

156. Many are thy mercies, O Lord; * revive me according to thy decrees.

157. Many are my persecutors and my enemies: * but I turn not aside from thy decrees.

158. I beheld the faithless and it wearied me, * because they kept not thy word.

159. See, O Lord, how I love thy precepts; * revive me, according to thy goodness.

160. The sum of thy word is truth, * and everlasting is every ordinance of thy justice.

Ps. 118, xi—Lost and alone in this awful solitude he pleads with the Lord: "Seek thy servant, for I have not forgotten thy commandments."

The Law Gives Joy and Help

PSALM 118, XI

PRINCES persecute me without cause, * but my heart stands in awe of thy words.

162. I rejoice in thy words, * as one who finds rich spoil.

163. Falsehood I hate and abhor; * thy law I love.

164. Seven times a day I praise thee * because of thy just judgments.

165. Great peace have they who love thy law, * and for them there is no stumbling block.

166. I hope for thy deliverance, O Lord, * and I keep thy commandments.

167. My soul observes thy decrees, * and loves them exceedingly.

168. I keep thy precepts and decrees, * because my entire conduct is present to thee.

169. Let my cry come unto thee, O Lord; * give me understanding according to thy word.

170. Let my prayer come before thee, * deliver me according to thy word.

171. Let my lips pour forth praise, * when thou shalt teach me thy statutes.

172. Let my tongue chant thy word, * for all thy commandments are just.

173. Let thy hand be ready to help me, * for I have chosen thy precepts.

174. I long for thy salvation, O Lord, * and thy law is my delight.

175. Let me live to praise thee, * and let thy ordinances help me.

176. If I go astray like a lost sheep, seek thy servant, * for I have not forgotten thy commandments.

Glory be to the Father, and to the Son,

and to the Holy Ghost.

As it was in the beginning, is now,

and ever shall be, world without end. Amen.

Ps. 109—The Messias, King, Priest and Judge is enthroned above the world holding the sceptre of power and the scales of His justice. With His right hand He blesses His dominion—the whole world. Adoring angels serve him.

Messias, King, Priest, Victor

PSALM 109

Vespers

THE Lord said to my Lord: "Sit thou at my right hand, * until I make thy enemies thy footstool."

2. From Sion the Lord will stretch forth the sceptre of thy power; * "Rule thou in the midst of thy enemies!

3. Royal power is thine on the day of thy birth in the splendor of holiness: * like dew before the day-star, have I begotten thee."

4. The Lord has sworn and he will not repent: * "Thou art a priest forever according to the order of Melchisedech."

5. The Lord is at thy right hand: * he will crush kings in the day of his wrath.

6. He will judge the nations, he will heap high corpses; * he will crush heads over a wide area.

7. From a brook by the wayside he will drink, * therefore will he lift up his head.

PSALM 110

Prayer After Holy Communion

I WILL thank the Lord with my whole heart, * in the circle of the just and in the congregation.

2. Great are the works of the Lord, * worthy of study for all who love them.

3. Splendid and glorious is his work; * and his justice abides forever.

4. He has left a memorial of his wonders; * merciful and kind is the Lord.

5. He has given food to those who fear him; * he will be mindful forever of his covenant.

6. He has shown his powerful works to his people, * in giving them possession of the nations.

Ps. 110—Israelites gather the heavenly manna before sunrise. This heavenly food is offered to God in praise and thanksgiving. "He has given food to those who fear him."

---

7. Trustworthy and just are the works of his hands; * grounded in truth are all his precepts.

8. Established forever and ever, * based on truth and equity.

9. He has sent deliverance to his people, he has established his covenant forever; * holy is his name and worthy of reverence.

10. The fear of the Lord is the beginning of wisdom: prudent is the conduct of all, who practise it; * his praise abides forever.

The Happiness of the Just Man

PSALM 111

HAPPY the man who fears the Lord, * who greatly delights in his commandments.

2. His descendants shall be powerful upon earth; * the offspring of the righteous shall be blessed.

3. Wealth and riches shall be in his house, * and his liberality shall endure forever.

4. He rises in the darkness, as a light to the upright, * kind and merciful and just.

5. Fortunate is the man who is kind and lends, * who conducts his business justly.

6. He shall never waver; * the just man shall be remembered forever.

7. He shall not fear sad news; * his heart is firm, trusting in the Lord.

8. His heart is steadfast, he shall not fear, * until he sees his enemies defeated.

9. He gives lavishly to the poor, his generosity shall endure forever; * his power shall rise in honor.

10. The wicked man shall see this and become indignant, he shall gnash his teeth and waste away; * the desire of the wicked shall perish.

Ps. 112—A great multitude of the faithful, praising the name of the Lord, advance in the procession of life, illuminated by Divine Light and blessed with goods and children pictured at right and left.

PSALM 112

A Call to Praise the Lord

PRAISE, O servants of the Lord, * praise the name of the Lord.

2. Blessed be the name of the Lord * both now and forever.

3. From sunrise to sunset * may the name of the Lord be praised.

4. The Lord is high above all nations, * his glory above the heavens.

5. Who is like the Lord, our God, who is

6. enthroned on high * and looks down upon heaven and earth.

7. He raises the needy from the dust, * he lifts up the poor man from the dunghill,

8. To place him with princes, * with the princes of his people.

9. He makes her, who was barren, to dwell in a home, * the joyful mother of children.

Deliverance from the Bondage of Sin

PSALM 113

WHEN Israel went forth from Egypt, * the house of Jacob from a people of alien tongue,

2. Juda became his sanctuary, * Israel his dominion.

3. The sea saw it and fled, * the Jordan turned back.

4. The mountains skipped like rams, * the hills like lambs.

5. What ails you, O sea, that you flee? * O Jordan, that you turn back?

6. O mountains, that you skip like rams, * O hills, like lambs?

7. Tremble, O earth, at the presence of the Lord, * at the presence of the God of Jacob.

8. Who turned the rock into a pool of water, * the flint-rock into flowing springs.

Ps. 113—*The chosen People leave Egypt. The patriarch in center, on camel, thanks God for the liberation of his people. Figure on right points to idols of the enemy. "They have eyes but see not; they have ears but hear not."*

---

9. Not to us, O Lord, not to us, but to thy name give glory, * because of thy mercy and thy faithfulness.

10. Why should the nations say: * "Where is their God?"

11. Our God is in heaven; * all that he willed, he has done.

12. Their idols are silver and gold, * the work of men's hands.

13. They have mouths, but speak not; * they have eyes, but see not.

14. They have ears, but hear not; * they have noses, but smell not.

15. They have hands, but feel not; they have feet but walk not; * they utter no sound with their throat.

16. Like to them shall they be, who make them, * everyone who trusts in them.

17. The house of Israel trusts in the Lord: * he is their helper and their shield.

18. The house of Aaron trusts in the Lord: * he is their helper and their shield.

19. They who fear the Lord, trust in the Lord * he is their helper and their shield.

20. The Lord remembers us * and will bless us;

He will bless the house of Israel, * he will bless the house of Aaron.

21. He will bless those who fear the Lord, * both little and great.

22. The Lord will grant you increase, * you and your children.

23. Blessed be you by the Lord, * who made heaven and earth.

24. Heaven is the heaven of the Lord, * but the earth he has given to men.

25. The dead do not praise the Lord, * nor anyone who goes down into silence.

26. But we bless the Lord, * both now and forever.

Ps. 4—In flight from his son, David pitches his tent in a desert place. Here he is saying his night prayer, confiding his night's rest to God. A guard watches outside.

Night Prayer

PSALM 4

Compline

ANSWER me, when I call, O my just God, thou who gavest me relief in my distress; * have pity on me and answer my prayer.

3. You men, how long will you be hard-hearted? * why do you love vanity and seek after falsehood?

4. Know that the Lord deals wonderfully with his holy one; * the Lord will hear when I call to him.

5. Tremble, and sin not, * ponder within your hearts, upon your beds, and be silent.

6. Offer fitting sacrifices, * and trust in the Lord.

7. Many say: "Who will show us good things?" * Let the light of thy countenance shine upon us, O Lord!

8. Thou hast given joy to my heart * greater than when men abound in corn and wine.

9. As soon as I lie down, I fall asleep in peace, for thou alone, O Lord, * dost make me dwell in security.

Night Prayer

PSALM 90

YOU who dwell in the shelter of the Most High, * who abide under the shadow of the Almighty,

2. Say to the Lord: "My refuge and my fortress, * my God, in whom I trust."

3. For he will deliver you from the snare of the fowlers, * from the deadly pestilence.

4. He will shelter you with his pinions, and you shall take refuge under his wings: * his fidelity is a shield and a buckler.

5. You shall fear neither the terror of night, * nor the arrow that flies by day,

Ps. 90—*The man who trusts in God is protected by Him from all evil spirits, dangers and attacks illustrated by the devil, the skeleton and the man in ambush.*

---

6. Nor the pestilence that creeps in darkness, * nor the plague that lays waste at noonday.

7. Though a thousand should fall at your side, and ten thousand at your right hand: * it shall not reach you.

8. But with your own eyes you shall see * and behold the punishment of the wicked.

9. For the Lord is your refuge, * you have made the Most High your defense.

10. No evil shall befall you, * no plague shall approach your dwelling,

11. Because he has given his angels charge over you, * to protect you in all your ways.

12. Upon their hands they shall bear you up, * lest you dash your foot against a stone.

13. You shall tread upon the asp and the viper, * you shall trample under foot the lion and the serpent.

14. Because he remained close to me, I will deliver him; * I will protect him, because he has known my name.

15. He shall call upon me and I will answer him; I will be with him in trouble, * I will rescue him and honor him.

16. With long life will I satisfy him, * and show him my salvation.

Night Prayer

PSALM 133

BEHOLD, bless the Lord, * all you servants of the Lord;

Who stand in the house of the Lord * during the night hours.

2. Lift up your hands toward the sanctuary * and bless the Lord.

3. May the Lord bless you from Sion, * he who made heaven and earth.

Glory be to the Father, and to the Son, and to the Holy Ghost . . .

Ps. 13—Men who deny God are a prey to the spirit of destruction, hate and envy; they set fire to the city and kill one another.

Evils of Unbelief; Their Punishment

I Nocturn **PSALM 13** Matins

THE fool says in his heart: * "There is no God." They are corrupt, they have done abominable things; * there is none who does good.

2. The Lord looks down from heaven upon men, * to see if there be one who is wise and seeks God.

3. All have gone astray together, all are perverted: * there is none who does good, not even one.

4. Will not all evildoers come to their senses, * who devour my people as they eat bread?

5. They did not call upon the Lord: they shall then tremble with fear, * for God is with the just generation.

6. You would confuse the counsel of the afflicted: * but the Lord is his refuge.

7. Oh, may the deliverance of Israel come from Sion! when the Lord shall restore the fortunes of his people, * Jacob shall be joyful, Israel shall rejoice.

The Ideal Man of God

PSALM 14

O LORD, who may be a guest in thy tabernacle, * who may dwell upon thy holy mountain?

2. He who lives blamelessly and practices justice and thinks truthfully in his heart, *

3. and has no slander on his tongue; Who does no evil to his fellow, * nor casts slurs upon his neighbor.

4. Who holds the sinner in disdain, * but honors those who fear the Lord;

5. Who, even if he swears to his own injury, retracts not, who puts not out his money for usury, * nor takes bribes against the innocent.

Whoever does these things, * shall never waver.

Ps. 16—"Guard me as the apple of thy eye, hide me under the shadow of thy wings from the wicked."

A Prayer for Justice Against Enemies

PSALM 16

HEAR, O Lord, my just plea, hearken to my cry, * listen to my prayer from lips without deceit.

2. Let my sentence proceed from thee: * thy eyes see what is right.

3. If thou test my heart, if thou examine it in the night, if thou prove me with fire, * thou wilt find no wickedness in me.

4. My mouth has not sinned after the manner of men; * according to the words of thy lips I have kept the ways of the law.

5. My steps have held fast to thy paths, * my feet have not slipped.

6. I call upon thee, for thou wilt answer me, O God; * incline thy ear to me, hear my utterance.

7. Show thy wonderful goodness, * thou who savest from their foes those who take refuge at thy right hand.

8. Guard me as the apple of thy eye, hide me under the shadow of thy wings, *

9. from the wicked who use violence against me.

My enemies surround me with fury,

10. they shut up their unfeeling heart, * with their mouth they speak arrogantly.

11. Now their steps surround me, * they watch intently to throw me to the ground,

12. Like a lion eager for prey, * and a young lion that lurks in ambush.

13. Arise, O Lord, confront him, cast him down, save my life from the wicked with thy sword, * with thy hand, O Lord, from men:

From men who have their reward in this life, * and whose belly thou fillest with thy treasures:

Whose sons are glutted * and they leave their inheritance to their children.

15. But as for me, in justice I shall behold thy face, * when I awake, I shall be satisfied with the vision of thee.

Ps. 17—"In my distress I called upon the Lord . . . and from his holy temple he heard my voice . . . he lowered the heavens and came down."

Prayer of Thanksgiving

PSALM 17, I

II Nocturn

I LOVE thee, O Lord, my strength, *
3. O Lord, my rock, my fortress, my deliverer.

My God, my rock of refuge, * my shield, the strength of my salvation, my stronghold!

4. I will call upon the Lord, most praiseworthy, * and I will be safe from my foes.

5. The waves of destruction engulfed me, * and the torrents of iniquity terrified me;

6. The bonds of hell surrounded me, * the snares of death enmeshed me.

7. In my distress I called upon the Lord, * and unto my God I cried out;

And from his temple he heard my voice, * and my cry came to his ears.

8. The earth shook and trembled, the foundations of the mountains quaked * and rocked, because he was burning with rage.

9. Smoke rose from his nostrils, and from his mouth a devouring fire, * fire-brands were enkindled by him.

10. He lowered the heavens and came down, * and a dark cloud was under his feet.

11. He rode upon a Cherub and he flew, * and he soared on the wings of the wind.

12. He put on darkness as a veil, * dark waters and dense clouds as his covering.

13. Because of the brightness of his face * burning coals were kindled.

14. And the Lord thundered from heaven, * and the Most High gave forth his voice.

15. And he sent forth his arrows and scattered them, * much lightning, and routed them.

16. Then the depths of the sea appeared * and the foundations of the world were laid bare

At the rebuke of the Lord, * at the blast of the breath of his wrath.

Ps. 17, ii—"He drew me out of many waters . . . and he led me forth into an open space, he saved me because he loves me."

Prayer of Thanksgiving

PSALM 17, II

HE reached forth from on high, he grasped me, * he drew me out of many waters.

18. He rescued me from my mighty foe, * and from my enemies, who were too strong for me.

19. They attacked me in the day of my misfortune, * but the Lord was my support,

20. And he led me forth into an open space, * he saved me, because he loves me.

21. The Lord dealt with me according to my righteousness, * according to the cleanness of my hands has he rewarded me,

22. For I have kept the ways of the Lord, * and have not departed from my God by sinning,

23. For I have kept all his ordinances before my eyes, * and his statutes I did not set aside.

24. But I stood before him without stain, * and kept myself from all fault.

25. So the Lord rewarded me according to my righteousness, * according to the cleanness of my hands in his sight.

26. With the kind thou showest thyself kind, * with the perfect thou dost act perfectly,

27. With the pure thou showest thyself pure, * but with the perverse thou dealest craftily.

28. For thou dost save an humble people, * but haughty eyes thou bringest low.

29. For thou dost light my lamp, O Lord; * my God, thou dost enlighten my darkness.

30. For through thee I can charge against armed forces, * and with the help of my God I can scale a fortress wall.

31. God's way is perfect, the word of the Lord is fire-tried; * he is a shield for all who take refuge in him.

Prayer of Thanksgiving

PSALM 17, III

FOR who is God but the Lord? * or who is a rock but our God.

33. The God who girded me with strength * and made my way perfect,

34. Who made my feet as fleet as the feet of stags, * and set me firmly upon high ground,

35. Who trained my hands for battle, * and my arms to bend the brazen bow.

36. And thou gavest me thy saving shield, thy right hand upheld me, * and thy care made me great.

37. Thou hast widened the way for my steps, * and my feet have not faltered.

38. I pursued my enemies and overtook them, * nor did I turn back, until I had slain them.

39. I smote them and they could not rise, * they fell beneath my feet.

40. For thou didst gird me with strength for battle, * and bend my adversaries beneath me.

41. For thou hast put my enemies to flight, * and scattered those who hated me.

42. They cried out—and there was none to save them; * unto the Lord—and he heard them not.

43. And I scattered them as dust before the wind, * I stamped them down as the dirt of the streets.

44. Thou hast delivered me from the strife of the people, * thou hast made me the head of the nations.

45. A people I knew not, became my servants, * they obeyed me, as soon as they heard of me.

46. Foreigners flattered me, foreigners grew pale, * they came out trembling from their fortresses.

47. The Lord lives, and blessed be my Rock, * my God, my savior, be exalted,

48. The God who has avenged me * and made peoples subject to me.

49. Thou who hast freed me from my foes, and raised me above my adversaries, * thou hast saved me from the man of violence.

50. Therefore will I praise thee among the nations, O Lord, * and chant a hymn to thy name:

51. Thou who hast granted great victories to the king and shown kindness to thy anointed, * to David and his descendants forever.

Ps. 19—"May we rejoice in thy victory, and raise banners in the name of our God."

Days of Distress, Days of Prayer

PSALM 19

III Nocturn

MAY the Lord answer thee in the day of trial, * may the name of the God of Jacob protect thee.

3. May he send thee help from the sanctuary, * and support thee from Sion.

4. May he be mindful of all thy offerings, * and accept thy burnt offering.

5. May he grant thee thy heart's desire, * and fulfill all thy plans.

6. May we rejoice in thy victory, and raise banners in the name of our God; * may the Lord grant all your requests!

7. Now I know the Lord has granted victory to his anointed, * that he has answered him from his

holy heaven with the might of his victorious right hand.

8. Some trust in chariots and some in horses, * but we are strong in the name of the Lord, our God.

9. They have tottered and fallen, * but we stand erect and remain.

10. O Lord, grant victory to the king, * and answer us, when we call upon thee.

Joyous Gratitude

PSALM 20

O LORD, the king is glad because of thy strength, * and because of thy help he rejoices exceedingly!

3. Thou hast given him his heart's desire, * and denied him not the request of his lips.

4. For thou comest to meet him with choice blessings, * thou hast set on his head a crown of fine gold.

5. He asked life of thee: thou gavest to him * length of days forever and ever.

6. Great is his glory because of thy help, * majesty and splendor hast thou conferred upon him.

7. Thou hast made him blessed forever, * thou hast gladdened him with joy in thy presence.

Ps. 20—*A prayer of thanksgiving for victory granted the king in battle.*

---

8. For the king trusts in the Lord, * and through the favor of the Most High he shall not waver.

9. May thy hand come upon all thy enemies: * may thy right hand reach all who hate thee

10. Put them as in a fiery furnace, * when thou dost appear.

May the Lord consume them in his wrath, * and fire devour them.

11. Root out their offspring from the earth, * and their descendants from among men.

12. Though they aim evil against thee, * and plot, they shall not prevail;

13. For thou shalt put them to flight, * thou shalt aim thy bow at their faces.

14. Arise, O Lord, in thy strength! * we will sing and praise thy power.

Prayer in Time of Sickness

PSALM 29

I WILL praise thee, O Lord, for thou hast delivered me, * and hast not let my enemies rejoice over me.

3. O Lord, my God, * I cried to thee, and thou didst heal me.

4. O Lord, thou hast brought forth my soul from the abyss; * thou hast saved me from those who go down into the pit.

5. Sing praises to the Lord, O you his faithful, * and give thanks to his holy name.

6. For his anger lasts but for a moment, * his benevolence for a lifetime.

Weeping comes in the evening, * but gladness in the morning.

7. Now in my confidence I said: * "I shall never waver"

8. O Lord, by thy favor thou hast given me honor and power; * when thou didst hide thy face, I became troubled.

9. To thee, O Lord, I cry, * and implore the mercy of my God:

Ps. 29—*Psalmist, threatened by death, thanks God for health restored. "O Lord, my God, I cried to thee, and thou didst heal me."*

10. "What profit will there be in my blood, * in my descent into the grave?

Shall the dust praise thee, * or declare thy faithfulness?

11. Hear, O Lord, and have pity on me; * Lord, be thou my helper.

12. Thou hast turned my mourning into dancing; * thou hast removed my garment of sorrow, and clad me with gladness:

13. So that my soul may sing praises to thee without ceasing, * O Lord, my God, forever will I praise thee.

A Summons to All Peoples to Acknowledge and Praise the Kingdom of God

PSALM 46

Lauds

ALL peoples, clap your hands, * shout to God with joyful voice,

3. For the Lord, most high, is awe-inspiring, * he is a great king over all the earth.

4. He makes peoples subject to us, * and puts nations under our feet.

5. He chooses our inheritance for us, * the glory of Jacob, whom he loves.

6. God has ascended amid jubilation, * the Lord with the sound of trumpets.

7. Sing praises to God, sing praises; * sing praises to our king, sing praises.

8. For God is king of all the earth, * sing a hymn.

9. God rules over all the nations, * God sits on his holy throne.

10. The princes of the peoples are assembled * with the people of the God of Abraham.

11. For the rulers of the earth belong to God: * he is exceedingly exalted.

Ps. 5,—*The Psalmist offers sacrifice. "I will bow down toward thy holy temple in reverence before thee, O Lord."*

Morning Prayer

PSALM 5

HEARKEN to my words, O Lord, * attend to my sighing.

3. Heed my cry for help, * my King and my God!

4. For to thee, O Lord, do I pray; in the morning thou hearest my voice; * in the morning I offer to thee my prayers and I wait.

5. For thou art not a God who delights in wickedness, nor may the wicked abide

6. with thee; * the arrogant may not stand in thy presence.

7. Thou hatest all evildoers, * thou destroyest all liars;

The man of blood and treachery * the Lord abominates.

8. But I, by thy abundant kindness, * will enter thy house,

I will bow down toward thy holy temple *

9. in reverence before thee, * O Lord.

Lead me in thy justice, because of my enemies; * make thy way straight before me.

10. For there is no sincerity in their speech; * their heart devises treachery;

Their throat is an open sepulchre; * they flatter with their tongues.

11. Punish them, O God, * let them fail in their plans;

Cast them out because of their many crimes, * for they are rebellious against thee.

12. But let all who take refuge in thee rejoice, * let them be glad forever.

And do thou protect them and let them rejoice in thee, * who love thy name.

13. For thou dost bless the just man, O Lord: * with thy benevolence, as with a shield thou dost surround him.

Ps. 28—*God's power in nature. "The voice of the Lord breaks the cedars, the voice of the Lord shatters the cedars of Lebanon."*

The Magnificence of God in a Storm

PSALM 28

ASCRIBE to the Lord, O sons of God, * ascribe to the Lord glory and power!

2. Ascribe to the Lord the glory due his name, * worship the Lord in holy attire.

3. The voice of the Lord is upon the waters! the God of majesty has thundered: * the Lord upon many waters.

4. Mighty is the voice of the Lord! * the voice of the Lord is full of majesty!

5. The voice of the Lord breaks the cedars, * the voice of the Lord shatters the cedars of Lebanon,

6. He makes Lebanon skip like a calf, * and Sarion like a young buffalo.

7. The voice of the Lord sends forth flames of fire, the voice of the Lord shakes the desert, * the Lord shakes the desert of Cades.

8. The voice of the Lord twists the oaks and strips bare the forests: * and in his temple all cry: Glory!

10. The Lord sat above the flood, * and the Lord presides as a king forever.

11. The Lord will give strength to his people, * the Lord will bless his people with peace.

Canticle of David

BLESSED art thou, O Lord, God of our father Israel, * from eternity to eternity.

11. Thine, O Lord are grandeur and power, * and splendor and glory and majesty.

For all that is in heaven and on earth is thine; * thine is the kingdom, O Lord, and thou art the ruler who is exalted above all.

12. Wealth and honor are from thee, * and by thy power thou rulest all things. And in thy hand are strength and power, * and to thy hand it belongs to make everything great and strong.

13. Now therefore, our God, we thank thee * and we praise thy glorious name.

Ps. 116—Calling upon all the world to praise God. "Praise the Lord all you nations, praise him, all you peoples."

A Short Act of Praise

PSALM 116

PRAISE the Lord, all you nations, * praise him, all you peoples,

2. For his goodness manifests itself to us mightily, * and the faithfulness of the Lord remains forever.

Glory be to the Father, and to the Son,

and to the Holy Ghost.

As it was in the beginning, is now,

and ever shall be, world without end. Amen.

Thoughts on God's Sanctuary

PSALM 23

Prime

THE earth is the Lord's and the fulness thereof, * the world and they who dwell therein.

2. For he has founded it upon the seas, * and has made it firm upon the floods.

3. Who may ascend the mountain of the Lord, * who may stand in his holy place?

4. He whose hands are pure, whose heart is clean, who has not set his mind on vain things, * nor sworn deceitfully to his neighbor.

5. He shall receive a blessing from the Lord * and a reward from God his Savior

6. Such is the generation of those who seek him, * who seek the face of the God of Jacob.

7. Lift up your heads, O gates; and lift yourselves up, O ancient portals, * that the king of glory may come in!

8. "Who is this king of glory?" * "The Lord, strong and mighty, the Lord, mighty in battle."

9. Lift up your heads, O gates; and lift yourselves up, O ancient portals, * that the king of glory may come in!

10. "Who is this king of glory?" * "The Lord of hosts: he is the king of glory."

Ps. 18, i—*"The heavens declare the glory of God and the firmament proclaims the work of his hands."*

Prayer to Obtain Love of God's Law

PSALM 18, I

THE heavens declare the glory of God, * and the firmament proclaims the work of his hands.

3. Day declares the message unto day, * and night unto night reveals this knowledge.

4. There is neither speech nor discourse, * their voice cannot be heard.

5. Yet they resound through all the earth, * and their words to the ends of the world. There he has set up his tabernacle for the

6. sun, which goes forth like a bride-groom from his chamber * and rejoices, like a giant, to run the course.

7. From one end of the heavens is its rising, and its course ends at the other, * nothing is hidden from its heat.

PSALM 18, II

THE law of the Lord is perfect, refreshing the soul; * the decree of the Lord is trustworthy, making wise the simple;

9. The precepts of the Lord are right, rejoicing the heart; * the commandment of the Lord is pure, enlightening the eyes;

10. The fear of the Lord is pure, enduring forever; * the judgments of the Lord are true, and wholly just,

11. They are more desirable than gold, and much fine gold, * and sweeter than honey and the honey comb.

12. Although thy servant heeds them, * and is most careful in observing them,

13. Who can know one's failures? * cleanse me from my hidden faults,

14. From pride also keep thy servant, * lest it rule over me.

Then shall I be blameless and free * from grievous sin.

15. May the words of my mouth and the thoughts of my heart be acceptable before thee, * O Lord, my Rock and my Redeemer.

Ps. 26, i—"The Lord is my light and my salvation: whom shall I fear?" "Though an army should encamp against me, my heart shall not fear."

Prayer of Confidence

PSALM 26, I

Terce

THE Lord is my light and my salvation: whom shall I fear? * The Lord is the defense of my life: whom shall I dread?

2. When evildoers assail me, to devour me, * my enemies and my foes, they stumble and fall.

3. Though an army should encamp against me, my heart shall not fear; * though war should rise against me, even then will I trust.

4. One thing I ask of the Lord, this do I seek: * that I may dwell in the house of the Lord all the days of my life,

To enjoy the graciousness of the Lord, * and to behold his temple.

5. For he will hide me in his tent in the day of adversity, * he will shelter me in the secret place of his tabernacle, he will set me high upon a rock.

6. Even now my head is lifted up * above my enemies round about me,

And I will offer joyful sacrifices in his tabernacle, * I will sing and chant praises to the Lord.

PSALM 26, II

HEAR, O Lord, my voice which cries to thee, * be gracious to me and answer me.

8. My heart speaks to thee, my face seeks thee; * thy face, O Lord, I seek.

9. Hide not thy face from me, * rebuff not thy servant in anger.

Thou art my help; cast me not off, * nor forsake me, O God, my savior.

10. Though my father and my mother abandon me, * yet will the Lord receive me.

11. Teach me thy way, O Lord, * and lead me along a safe path because of my enemies.

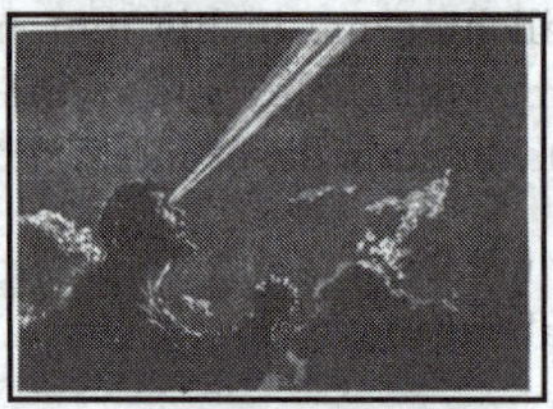

Ps. 26, ii—"My heart speaks to thee, my face seeks thee; thy face, O Lord, do I seek."

---

12. Deliver me not to the desires of my foes, * for false witnesses have risen up against me, and men who breathe violence.
13. I believe that I shall behold the goodness of the Lord * in the land of the living.
14. Wait for the Lord, be strong, * and let thy heart take courage, and wait for the Lord.

An Earnest Prayer for Protection Against Enemies

PSALM 27

UNTO thee do I cry, O Lord; * my rock, be not deaf to me,

Lest, if thou hear me not, I become like * unto them who go down into the pit.

2. Hear the voice of my pleading, when I cry to thee, * when I lift up my hands to thy holy temple.

3. Drag me not away with sinners * and evildoers,

Who speak amicably with their neighbors, * but harbor evil in their hearts.

4. Render to them according to their deeds * and according to their evil actions. Render to them according to the work of their hands, * pay back to them what they have done.

5. Because they heed not the deeds of the Lord nor the work of his hands, * may he destroy them and not build them up again.

6. Blessed be the Lord, for he has heard

7. the voice of my pleading, * the Lord, my strength and my shield!

My heart trusted in him and I was helped; * therefore my heart rejoices, and I praise him with my song.

8. The Lord is strength to his people, * a stronghold of salvation to his anointed.

9. Save thy people, and bless thy inheritance * and shepherd them and carry them forever.

Ps. 30, i—"To thee, O Lord, I flee for refuge . . . Thou wilt bring me out of the net they have hidden for me."

Acts of Confidence

PSALM 30, I

Sext

TO thee, O Lord, I flee for refuge: let me never be put to shame; * in thy justice deliver me!

3. Incline thy ear to me, * make haste to rescue me.

Be to me a rock of refuge, * a fortress to save me.

4. For thou art my rock and my stronghold, * and for thy name's sake thou wilt lead me and guide me.

5. Thou wilt bring me out of the net which they have hidden for me, * for thou art my refuge.

6. Into thy hands I commend my spirit: * thou wilt redeem me, O Lord, faithful God.

7. Thou hatest the worshippers of empty idols; * but I trust in the Lord.
8. I will be glad and rejoice because of thy kindness, for thou hast seen my misery, * and in my distress thou hast helped me.
9. Thou hast not delivered me into the power of the enemy, * but thou hast set my feet in a spacious place.

Confident Prayer in Distress

PSALM 30, II

HAVE pity on me, O Lord, for I am in trouble; * my eye grows weak with grief, my soul and my body.
11. For my life is spent in sorrow, * my years in groaning.
My strength has failed through affliction, * and my bones have wasted away.
12. I have become an object of scorn to all my enemies, a mockery to my neighbors, and an object of terror to my friends, * they who see me in public, flee from me.
13. I am fully forgotten, as one dead, * I am like a broken vessel.
14. For I have heard the whispering of the crowd—terror is everywhere! * plotting against me, they plan to take my life.

Ps. 30, ii—*"Have pity on me, O Lord . . . I have become an object of scorn to all my enemies, a mockery to my neighbors . . . But I trust in thee, O Lord; I say: Thou art my God."*

---

15. But I trust in thee, O Lord: * I say: Thou art my God.

16. My destiny is in thy hand: * deliver me from the power of my foes and persecutors.

17. Look favorably upon thy servant, * save me in thy mercy.

18. O Lord, let me not be put to shame: for I have called upon thee; * let the wicked be put to shame, let them be silenced, cast down into the abyss.

19. Let lying lips become dumb, * which in pride and scorn speak arrogantly against the just man.

Ps. 30, iii—"Blessed be the Lord, for he has shown me his marvelous mercy."

Prayer Answered: Deep Gratitude

PSALM 30, III

HOW great is thy goodness, O Lord, * which thou hast reserved for those who fear thee,

Which thou showest to them who have recourse to thee, * in the sight of men.

21. Thou shieldest them with thy presence * from the conspiracies of men.

Thou hidest them in thy tent * from the wrangling of tongues.

22. Blessed be the Lord, for he has shown me * his marvelous mercy in a fortified city.

23. Yet I said in my anxiety: * "I am cut off from thy sight:"

But thou hast heard the voice of my pleading, * when I cried to thee.

24. Love the Lord, all his devoted servants! * the Lord guards the faithful,

But he repays fully * those who act haughtily.

25. Take courage and let your heart be strengthened, * all who hope in the Lord.

Act of Thanksgiving After Confession

PSALM 31

None

HAPPY is he whose iniquity is forgiven, * whose sin is pardoned.

2. Happy the man to whom the Lord imputes no guilt, * and in whose spirit there is no deceit.

3. As long as I was silent, my bones wasted away * amid my continual groanings.

4. For day and night thy hand lay heavy upon me, * my strength was sapped as with summer heat.

5. My sin I confessed to thee, * and my guilt I did not hide;

I said: I confess my iniquity to the Lord, * and thou didst forgive the guilt of my sin.

Ps. 31—A picture of the contrite soul freed from the thorn-like sting of a guilty conscience and restored to friendship with God.

---

6. Therefore every pious man will pray to thee * in time of need.

When the floods rush in, * they will not reach him.

7. Thou art a refuge to me, thou wilt guard me against distress, * with the joy of my salvation thou wilt surround me.

8. I will instruct thee, and direct thee in the way thou shouldst walk; * I will counsel thee, and keep my eyes fixed upon thee.

9. Be not like the horse and the mule, without understanding, whose temper is curbed by bit and bridle, * else they will not approach thee.

10. Many are the sorrows of the wicked; * but kindness surrounds him who hopes in the Lord.

11. Be glad in the Lord, and rejoice, you just; * and be jubilant, all you upright of heart.

A Splendid Poem of Praise, Thanksgiving and Confidence

PSALM 32, I

REJOICE in the Lord, you just; * praise befits the righteous.

2. Give thanks to the Lord on the lyre, * sing praises to him on the ten-stringed harp.

3. Sing to him a new canticle, * play skilfully to him amid shouts of joy.

4. For the word of the Lord is right, * and all his work trustworthy.

5. He loves justice and equity: * the earth is full of the goodness of the Lord.

6. By the word of the Lord the heavens were made, * and all the host thereof by the breath of his mouth.

7. He gathers together the waters of the sea as in a bottle: * he places the oceans in storehouses.

Ps. 32, i—Divine Providence reigning over the universe. "The earth is full of the goodness of the Lord."

8. Let all the earth fear the Lord: * and all dwellers on earth stand in awe of him.

9. For he spoke, and they were made; * he commanded, and they came into being.

10. The Lord brings to naught the counsel of the nations; * he thwarts the designs of the peoples.

11. The plan of the Lord remains forever: * the designs of his heart from age to age.

12. Blessed is the nation, whose God is the Lord; * the people whom he has chosen for his own inheritance.

God's Loving Kindness

PSALM 32, II

THE Lord looks from heaven: * he sees all the children of men.

14. From his dwelling-place he gazes upon * all the inhabitants of the earth:

15. He who has fashioned the hearts of all, * who takes note of all their deeds.

16. The king does not conquer by a large army: * the warrior is not saved by his great strength.

17. A horse is futile for victory, * and with all its strength, it does not afford escape.

18. Behold, the eyes of the Lord rest upon those who fear him: * on those who hope in his goodness,

19. That he may deliver their souls from death * and keep them alive in time of famine.

20. Our soul waits for the Lord: * he is our help and our shield.

21. In him, therefore, our heart rejoices, * in his holy name we trust.

22. Let thy mercy, O Lord, be upon us, * according as we hope in thee!

Ps. 114—*The Psalmist expresses his love for God and prays to be delivered from death that is already at the door.*

Prayer After Dangerous Illness

PSALM 114

Vespers

I LOVE the Lord: because he has heard * the voice of my pleading,

2. Because he inclined his ear to me, * when I called upon him.

3. The fetters of death encircled me, and the snares of hell seized upon me, * I fell into distress and sorrow.

4. But I called upon the name of the Lord: "O, Lord, save my life!"

5. The Lord is gracious and just, * and your God is merciful.

6. The Lord guards the simple: * I was helpless and he saved me.

7. Return, O my soul, to your rest, * for the Lord has dealt kindly with you.
8. For he has rescued me from death, * my eyes from tears, my feet from stumbling.
9. I shall walk before the Lord * in the land of the living.

A Prayer of Thanksgiving

PSALM 115

I TRUSTED, even when I said: "I am greatly afflicted;"
2. I said in my fear: * "Every man is deceitful!"
3. How shall I repay the Lord * for all his benefits to me?
4. I will take the chalice of salvation * and will call on the name of the Lord.
5. I will pay my vows to the Lord * in the presence of all his people.
6. Precious in the sight of the Lord * is the death of his saints.
7. O Lord, I am thy servant, I am thy servant, the son of thy handmaid: * thou hast loosed my bonds.
8. I will offer thee the sacrifice of praise, * and will call on the name of the Lord.
9. I will pay my vows to the Lord * in the presence of all his people.

Ps. 119—The Psalmist among a hostile people appeals to God for help.

10. In the courts of the house of the Lord, * in the midst of thee, O Jerusalem.

Prayer Against Evil Tongues

PSALM 119

IN my distress I cried to the Lord, * and he answered me.

2. O Lord, deliver me from lying lips, * from the deceitful tongue.

3. What shall *God* give to thee or what shall he add to thee, o deceitful tongue?

4. The sharp arrows of the warrior, * and the glowing embers of the broom-plant.

5. Woe is me, that I tarry in Mosoch, * that I dwell in the tents of Cedar!

6. Too long have I dwelt * with them, who hate peace.

7. When I speak of peace, * they want war.

Confidence in God's Protection

PSALM 120

I LIFT up my eyes to the mountains: * whence shall help come to me?

2. My help is from the Lord, * who made heaven and earth.

3. He will not suffer your foot to stumble, * your guardian will not slumber.

4. Behold, he will neither slumber nor sleep, * who guards Israel.

5. The Lord is your guardian, * the Lord is your protection at your right hand.

6. The sun shall not strike you by day, * nor the moon by night.

7. The Lord shall keep you from evil: * he shall guard your life.

8. The Lord shall guard your going and your coming, * henceforth and forever.

Ps. 121—*The pilgrims in sight of the Holy City. Some separate themselves from the caravan and from Mt. Olivet enjoy the panorama of Jerusalem: holy, beautiful, powerful.*

A Prayer for the Peace and Security of the Church

PSALM 121

I REJOICED when they said to me: * "We will go to the house of the Lord."

2. Our feet are even now standing * within thy gates, O Jerusalem,

3. Jerusalem built as a city, * so compact, so complete.

4. Thither the tribes go up, the tribes of the Lord, * according to the law of Israel, to give thanks to the name of the Lord.

5. There the thrones of judgment are set, * the thrones of the house of David.

Ps. 6—*At night when everything is lost in darkness, conscience is more awake than ever; David upon his bed cries and gives free vent to his repentance, praying for divine forgiveness.*

---

6. Pray for the peace of Jerusalem! * may they be safe who love thee!
7. May peace be within thy walls, * security within thy palaces!
8. For the sake of my brethren and my friends, * I will exclaim: peace be with thee!
9. For the sake of the house of the Lord, our God, * I will invoke blessings upon thee.

A Plea for Mercy in Time of Distress

PSALM 6

Compline

O LORD, reprove me not in thy anger, * nor chastise me in thy wrath.
3. Have pity on me, O Lord, for I am weak; * heal me, O Lord, for my very bones are shaken,

4. And my soul is deeply troubled; * but thou, O Lord, how long . . . ?

5. Return, O Lord, and save my life, * rescue me for thy mercy's sake.

6. For in death no one remembers thee: * who praises thee in the abode of the dead?

7. I am worn out with my sighing, night after night I moisten my bed with weeping, * with tears I drench my couch.

8. My eye is dim because of grief, * has grown old because of all my enemies.

9. Depart from me, all you evildoers, * for the Lord has heard my tearful cry.

10. The Lord has heard my pleading, * the Lord has accepted my prayer.

11. Let all my foes be brought to shame and utter confusion; * let them turn back and speedily be brought to shame.

An Appeal to God's Justice when Falsely Accused

PSALM 7, I

O LORD, my God, to thee do I flee for refuge; * save me from all my persecutors and deliver me;

3. Lest any one like a lion snatch my life, * and mangle me, with none to save me.

4. O Lord, my God, if I have done this, * if there is crime on my hands,

5. If I have done evil to my friend, * I, who have saved my unjust oppressors:

6. Let the enemy pursue and overtake me, trample my life to the ground, * and drag down my honor to the dust.

7. Arise, O Lord in thy anger, rise up against the madness of my oppressors, * and rise in my behalf at the judgment thou hast decreed.

8. Let the assembly of the nations gather about thee, * and sit thou above them on high.

9. The Lord is judge over the nations: judge me, O Lord, according to my righteousness * and the innocence, that is mine.

10. Let the malice of the wicked cease and do thou strengthen the just man, * O just God, searcher of heart and mind.

PSALM 7, II

A SHIELD for me is God, * who saves the upright of heart.

12. A just judge is God, * and a God who threatens every day.

13. Unless sinners be converted, he will sharpen his sword, * bend his bow and aim it.

Ps. 7, i—David fleeing from human injustice, calls upon Divine Justice. Saul's soldiers are at the foot of the hill.

---

14. And he will prepare deadly weapons for them, * he will make his arrows things of fire.

15. Behold, *the sinner* has conceived evil * and is in labor with malice and brings forth deceit.

16. He has dug a ditch and made it deep, * but he has fallen into the pit that he made.

17. His mischief will recoil upon his own head, * upon the crown of his head his violence will fall.

18. I will praise the Lord for his justice, * and sing praise to the name of the Lord Most High.

Glory be to the Father, and to the Son,
and to the Holy Ghost.
As it was in the beginning, is now,
and ever shall be, world without end. Amen.

Ps. 34, i—David appeals to God against the injustice and malice of his foes. "Let their way be dark and slippery, when the angel of the Lord pursues them."

Prayers for Those Who Suffer from False Accusations

I Nocturn **PSALM 34, I** Matins

OPPOSE, O Lord, those who oppose me, * fight against those who fight against me.

2. Take hold of shield and buckler, * and rise up to help me.

3. Brandish the spear and hold back my pursuers, * say to me: "I am thy salvation."

4. Let them be put to shame and confusion who seek my life, * let them be turned back and brought to shame who plan evil against me.

5. Let them be as chaff before the wind, * when the angel of the Lord drives them along.

6. Let their way be dark and slippery, * when the angel of the Lord pursues them.

7. For without cause they have laid their net for me, * without cause they have dug a pit for me.

8. May ruin come upon them unawares, and may they be caught in the net which they themselves have laid: * and may they fall into the pit they dug.

9. But my soul shall rejoice in the Lord, * and shall be glad because of his help.

10. All the powers of my being shall say: * "O Lord, who is like unto thee,

Thou savest the weak from the strong, * the needy and the poor from the robber."

The Ungrateful

PSALM 34, II

VIOLENT witnesses rose up! * they questioned me about things I knew not.

12. They repaid me with evil for good: * leaving my soul desolate.

13. But when they were sick, I put on the garment of mourning, afflicted myself with fasting, * and from within poured forth prayers.

Ps. 34, ii—*David seated at the doorstep bowed in grief. "They slandered me without ceasing; they tried me, they mocked me."*

---

14. I went about grieving as for a friend, or my own brother * I was bowed in sorrow as one mourning a mother.

15. Yet when I fell, they rejoiced and gathered, * they gathered against me, striking me unawares.

16. They slandered me without ceasing; they tried me, they mocked me, * they gnashed their teeth at me.

17. O Lord, how long wilt thou look on? * Save my soul from the roaring beasts, my life from the lions.

Ps. 34, iii—All good men will rejoice at the Psalmist's vindication and praise the justice of God.

The Arrogant

PSALM 34, III

I WILL give thee thanks in the great assembly, * I will praise thee amid a multitude of people.

19. Let not those who are unjustly my enemies rejoice over me; * nor let those who hate me without cause cast mocking glances at me.

20. For they do not speak of peace, * but they plan treacherous deeds against the peaceful citizens of the land.

21. They open wide their mouth against me, * they say, "Ha, ha! our eyes have seen it!"

22. Thou hast seen it, O Lord! Be not silent, * Lord, be not far from me!

23. Bestir thyself, and rise to my defense, * my God, and my Lord, to take up my cause.

24. Judge me according to thy justice, O Lord; * my God, let them not rejoice over me!

25. Let them not say to themselves: "Ah! Just what we wanted!" let them not say: "We have devoured him."

26. Let all of them together be put to shame and disgraced, * who rejoice at my misfortunes;

Let them be covered with confusion and dishonor, * who act insolently against me.

27. Let them rejoice and be glad who favor my cause, * and let them say always:

"The Lord be exalted, * who delights in the welfare of his servant."

28. And my tongue shall proclaim thy justice, * thy praise forever.

The Prosperity of the Wicked is Passing. The Happiness of the Just is Enduring.

PSALM 36, I

II Nocturn

BE not incensed because of evildoers, * nor envious of those who work iniquity;

2. For like grass they will soon wither * and like green herbs they will fade.

Ps. 36, i—David counsels the poor not to envy the rich and the evildoer. "For like grass they will soon wither . . . Hope in the Lord . . . and he shall grant you your heart's desire."

3. Hope in the Lord and do good, * that you may dwell in the land and enjoy security.

4. Seek your delight in the Lord, * and he shall grant you your heart's desire.

5. Entrust your life to the Lord, * hope in him and he will act.

6. And he will make your goodness shine like the light, * and the justice of your cause shine as the noonday.

7. Rest in the Lord, * and hope in him.

Be not incensed because of him who prospers in his undertakings, * because of one who plots evil things.

8. Refrain from anger and put aside wrath; * be not incensed, lest you do evil.

9. For evildoers shall be destroyed; * but they who hope in the Lord shall possess the land.

10. Yet a little while and the wicked shall be no more; * and if you look for his place, he shall not be there.

11. But the meek shall possess the land, * and shall delight in the fulness of peace.

12. The wicked man schemes against the just one * and gnashes his teeth at him.

13. The Lord laughs at him, * for he sees that his day is coming.

14. The wicked draw the sword, and bend their bow, to strike down the needy and the poor, * to slay those who walk in the right path.

15. Their sword shall pierce their own hearts, * and their bows shall be broken.

Earthly Prosperity Short-lived

PSALM 36, II

BETTER is the scanty store of the righteous, * than the great wealth of sinners;

17. For the strength of the wicked shall be broken, * but the Lord supports the just.

18. The Lord takes care of the life of the upright, * and their inheritance shall be forever.

Ps. 36, ii—In time of want the door of the wicked is closed to human misery, "but the just man is charitable and gives."

---

19. They shall not be put to shame in the time of disaster, * and in the days of famine they shall be satiated.

20. For the wicked shall perish and the Lord's enemies shall pass away like the beauty of the meadows, * they shall vanish like smoke.

21. The wicked man borrows and does not repay, * but the just man is charitable and gives.

22. For they whom the Lord blesses shall possess the land, * but they whom he curses shall perish.

23. A man's steps are made firm by the Lord, * and the conduct of such a one is pleasing to him.

24. Even though he falls, he does not remain prostrate, * for the Lord upholds his hand.

25. I was young, but now I am old, yet never have I seen the just forsaken, * nor his children begging bread.
26. At all times he is charitable and lends; * and his descendants shall be blessed.
27. Turn away from evil and do good, * that you may abide forever.
28. For the Lord loves justice, * and does not abandon his holy ones.
The wicked shall be destroyed, * and the offspring of the wicked shall be cut off.
29. The just shall possess the land * and shall dwell therein forever.

PSALM 36, III

THE mouth of the just speaks wisdom, * and his tongue says what is right.
31. The law of his God is in his heart, * and his steps do not falter.
32. The wicked man spies on the just, * and seeks to kill him.
33. The Lord will not leave him in his power, * nor let him be condemned when he is judged.
34. Trust in the Lord, * and follow his path: And he will exalt you, so that you shall possess the land; * with joy you shall see the destruction of the wicked.

35. I have seen the wicked man in his pride, * spreading himself like a leafy cedar.

36. And I passed by, and lo, he was no more; * and I sought him, but he was not to be found.

37. Mark the upright and consider the just man: * for there is a progeny for the man of peace.

38. But sinners shall all be destroyed, * the progeny of the wicked shall be cut off.

39. The salvation of the just is from the Lord; * he is their refuge in time of trouble.

40. And the Lord helps them and delivers them; * he frees them from the wicked and saves them, because they take refuge in him.

Ps. 37, i—"Rebuke me not, O Lord, in thy anger. Thy hand has come down upon me."

Penitential Prayer of a Sick Person

PSALM 37, I

III Nocturn

REBUKE me not, O Lord, in thy anger, * nor chastise me in thy wrath.

3. For thy arrows have pierced me, * and thy hand has come down upon me.

4. There is no soundness in my flesh because of thy wrath, * there is no health in my bones because of my sin.

5. For my guilt has overwhelmed me, * like a heavy load it weighs me down.

6. My wounds are foul and festering * because of my folly.

7. I am bent, I am bowed down exceedingly, * all day long I go about mourning.

8. For my loins are filled with burning pains, * and there is nothing healthy in my flesh.
9. I am benumbed and badly crushed, * I cry aloud because of the wild surging of my heart.
10. All my desire is known to thee, O Lord, * and my sighing is not hidden from thee.
11. My heart throbs, my strength is leaving me, * and the very light of my eyes fails me.
12. My friends and my companions stand aloof from my affliction, * and my relatives stand afar off.
13. They who seek my life lay snares, and they who seek to injure me threaten ruin, * and scheme treachery all day long.

God Our Only Refuge

PSALM 37, II

BUT I, like one deaf, hear not, * and I am like a dumb man who opens not his mouth.
15. And I am like a man who hears not, * and like one in whose mouth there is no retort.
16. For in thee, O Lord, I trust: * thou wilt answer me, O Lord, my God.
17. For I say: "Let them not rejoice over me; * when my foot slips, let them not become arrogant towards me."

Ps. 37, ii—*In his sickness and distress, while his friends and relatives stand afar off, David prays: "In thee, O Lord, I trust: thou wilt answer me, O Lord, my God."*

---

18. For I am ready to fall, * and my grief is ever with me.

19. For I confess my guilt, * and I am uneasy because of my sin.

20. But powerful are they who oppose me without reason, * and numerous are they who hate me unjustly;

21. And they who repay evil for good, * are my foes, because I seek to do good.

22. Forsake me not, O Lord, * my God, be not far from me!

23. Hasten to help me, * O Lord, my salvation!

Ps. 38—"Man passes away like a mere shadow . . . Turn thy angry eyes from me . . . before I depart and be no more."

Prayer in Time of Sickness for Patience and Resignation

I SAID: I will guard my ways, * lest I sin with my tongue;

I will put a bridle on my mouth, * while the wicked man stands before me.

3. I kept complete silence and had no comfort, * my pain was even increased.

4. My heart grew hot within me as I reflected, fire burst into flame: * I spoke with my tongue.

5. Lord, let me know my end, and what is the length of my days, * that I may know how frail I am.

6. Behold, thou hast made my days but a short span, and my life is as nothing before thee: * every man is but a breath.

7. Man passes away like a mere shadow, fruitless is all his worrying; * he hoards and knows not who shall enjoy these things.

8. And now what can I expect, O Lord? * my hope is in thee.

9. Deliver me from all my sins, * make me not the reproach of the fool.

10. I am dumb and open not my mouth: * for thou hast done it.

11. Remove thy scourge from me: * I am perishing under the blows of thy hand.

12. By punishing man's guilt, thou dost correct him; like a moth, thou dost consume his precious life: * every man is but a breath.

13. Hear my prayer, O Lord, listen to my cry, * be not indifferent to my tears.

14. For I am thy guest, * a pilgrim like all my fathers.

15. Turn thy angry eyes from me, that I may be refreshed, * before I depart and be no more.

Ps. 95—"Offer sacrifice and enter his courts; worship the Lord in holy attire."

Let All Praise the Lord

PSALM 95

Lauds

SING to the Lord a new song, * sing to the Lord, all the earth.

2. Sing to the Lord, bless his name, * proclaim his salvation day after day.

3. Declare his glory among the nations, * his wonders among all peoples.

4. For great is the Lord and highly to be praised, * to be feared above all the gods.

5. For all the gods of the heathen are vain idols; * but the Lord made the heavens.

6. Majesty and beauty are before him; * power and splendor are in his sanctuary.

7. Ascribe to the Lord, O families of the peoples, ascribe to the Lord glory and power; *

8. ascribe to the Lord the glory due his name.

Offer sacrifice and enter his courts; *

9. worship the Lord in holy attire.

Tremble before him, all the earth; *

10. proclaim among the nations: the Lord is king.

He has established the world, that it be not moved: * he rules the people with equity.

11. Let the heavens rejoice, and the earth be glad; let the sea and all that it contains

12. resound; * let the fields exult and all that is in them.

Then shall all the trees of the forest rejoice

13. before the Lord, for he comes, * for he comes to rule the earth.

He will rule the world with justice, * and the peoples according to his faithfulness.

Ardent Desire for the House of God

PSALM 42

VINDICATE me, O God, and plead my cause against a godless nation; * deliver me from the deceitful and wicked man.

Ps. 42—*The Psalmist, in exile and surrounded by hostile strangers, longs for the sanctuary. He prays and is confident that once again he will go to the altar of God.*

---

2. For thou, O God, art my strength: * why hast thou rejected me? why must I go about sorrowful, afflicted by the enemy?

3. Send forth thy light and thy truth: let them lead me, * let them bring me to thy holy mountain and to thy tabernacles.

4. Then I will go to the altar of God, * to God who is my joy and my gladness. *

And I will praise thee upon the lyre, * O God, my God!

5. Why art thou dejected, O my soul, * and disturbed within me?

Hope in God: for I shall again praise him, * my savior and my God.

Ps. 66—*Calling upon all men and nations to praise and thank God for the abundant harvest. "The earth has yielded its fruit: God, our God, has blessed us."*

A Prayer for the Missions

PSALM 66

MAY God be gracious to us and bless us; * may he look with favor upon us,

3. That men may know his way on earth, * his saving power among all nations.

4. May the peoples give thanks to thee, O God, * may all the peoples give thanks to thee.

5. May the nations be glad and rejoice, for thou judgest the peoples justly * and rulest the nations on earth.

6. May the peoples give thanks to thee, O God * may all the peoples gives thanks to thee.

7. The earth has yielded its fruit: * God, our God, has blessed us.

8. May God bless us, * and may all the ends of the earth fear him.

Whole-hearted Conversion to God

Canticle of Tobias

BLESSED be God, who lives for all eternity, * and his kingdom endures forever.

2. For he scourges and he has pity, he leads down to the abyss and brings back again: * nor can anyone escape his hand.

3. Give thanks to him, you children of Israel, in the presence of the nations: * for he has scattered us among them.

4. Show there his greatness, * utter his praises before all the living.

For he is our Lord and God, * he is our father forever.

5. He punishes us for our sins; and again he will have pity and will gather you together from all the nations, * among whom you were scattered.

6. If you shall be converted to him with your whole heart and all your soul, * so as to act sincerely before him,

Canticle of Tobias—*Tobias and his son gaze in wonderment, after the Archangel Raphael had revealed himself and then departed.*

Then will he return to you, * and he will not hide his face from you.

7. And consider, what he is about to do for you, * and give him thanks with the fulness of your voice.

And bless the just Lord, * and praise the eternal king.

8. I thank him in the land of my captivity, * and I show his power and greatness to a sinful nation.

Be converted, you sinners, and do what is right before him; * perhaps he will be kind to you and will show you mercy.

9. I will utter the praises of my God and of the king of heaven, * and my soul shall rejoice because of his greatness.

Praise God for His Many Benefits to Us

PSALM 134

PRAISE the name of the Lord; * praise it, you servants of the Lord,

2. Who stand in the house of the Lord, * in the courts of the house of our God.

3. Praise the Lord, for the Lord is good; * sing praise to his name, for it is sweet.

4. For the Lord has chosen Jacob for himself, * Israel for his own possession.

5. Truly I know this: the Lord is great, * and our Lord is above all gods.

6. Whatever the Lord wills, he does in heaven and on earth, * in the sea and in all the depths of the sea.

7. He brings up clouds from the ends of the earth, he makes the rain *follow* the lightning flashes, * he brings forth the winds from his storehouses.

He struck the first-born of Egypt, * men as well as beasts.

9. He produced signs and wonders in you, O Egypt, * against Pharaoh and all his servants.

10. He struck many nations * and slew mighty kings:

11. Sehon, king of the Amorites, and Og, king of Basan, * and all the kings of Canaan.

12. And he gave their land as a possession, * as a possession to Israel, his people.

13. Thy name, O Lord, endures for ever, * the memory of thee from age to age.

14. For the Lord protects his people, * and is gracious to his servants.

15. The idols of the nations are silver and gold, * the works of men's hands:

16. They have a mouth, but speak not; * they have eyes, but see not;

17. They have ears, but hear not; * and there is no breath in their mouth.

18. Like unto them are they who make them, * everyone who trusts in them.

19. O house of Israel, bless the Lord; * O house of Aaron, bless the Lord.

20. O house of Levi, bless the Lord; * you who worship the Lord, bless the Lord.

21. Blessed be the Lord from Sion, * he who dwells in Jerusalem.

Prayer for Guidance and Pardon

PSALM 24, I

Prime

TO thee, I lift up my soul, * O Lord, my God.
2. In thee I trust: let me not be put to shame! * let not my foes triumph over me!

Ps. 24, i—"To thee, I lift up my soul, O Lord, my God . . . let not my foes triumph over me."

---

3. Indeed, no one who hopes in thee shall be put to shame; * they shall be put to shame, who rashly break faith with thee.

4. Show me thy ways, O Lord, * and teach me thy paths.

5. Guide me in thy truth and teach me, for thou art God my savior: * and in thee I trust always.

6. Remember, O Lord, thy deeds of mercy * and thy acts of kindness, that are from eternity.

7. Remember not the sins of my youth and my offenses; according to thy mercy remember thou me, * for thy goodness' sake, O Lord.

PSALM 24, II

GRACIOUS and just is the Lord: * therefore he teaches sinners the right way.

9. He guides the lowly in justice, * he teaches the humble his way.

10. All the paths of the Lord are kindness and faithfulness * for those who keep his covenant and his precepts.

11. For thy name's sake, O Lord, * pardon my sin which is great.

12. Who is the man who fears the Lord? * he shall be taught what path to choose.

13. Such a one shall enjoy good fortune, * and his descendants shall possess the land.

14. The Lord is a friend to those who fear him, * and he makes his covenant known to them.

PSALM 24, III

MY eyes are ever turned towards the Lord, * for he will draw my feet out of the snare.

16. Look upon me and pity me, * for I am alone and afflicted.

17. Relieve the anguish of my heart, * and free me from my worries.

18. Behold my misery and my pain, * and forgive me all my sins.

19. Look at my foes: for they are many, * and they hate me vehemently.

20. Guard my life and rescue me, * lest I be put to shame for having sought refuge in thee.

21. May innocence and goodness guard me, * for I hope in thee, O Lord.

22. Deliver Israel, O God, * from all its troubles.

Ps. 39, i—David presses to his heart the sacred scroll—the Law. "To do thy will, O my God, is my delight, and thy law is in my very heart."

Thanksgiving for God's Mercies

PSALM 39, I

Terce

I PLACED firm confidence in the Lord, and he bent down to me, * and heard my cry.

3. He drew me out of the pit of destruction, out of the filthy mire; and he set my feet upon a rock, * and strengthened my steps.

4. He put into my mouth a new song, * a song of praise to our God.

Many shall see and fear, * and shall trust in the Lord.

5. Happy the man who has put his trust in the Lord, * and who follows not idolaters and apostates.

6. Many are the marvelous works thou hast done, O Lord, my God, * and in thy designs toward

us there is none like thee. Should I wish to proclaim and tell them, * they are more than can be numbered.

7. Sacrifice and oblation thou wouldst not, * but thou hast opened my ears.

Burnt-offering and sin-offering thou didst

8. not require: * then I said: "Behold I come; in the book it is written of me:

9. To do thy will, O my God, is my delight, * and thy law is in my very heart."

Gratitude in Action

PSALM 39, II

I HAVE proclaimed thy justice in the great assembly; * behold, I have not restrained my lips; Lord, thou knowest.

11. I have not concealed thy justice within my heart; * I have declared thy faithfulness and thy help.

I have not kept thy mercy * and faithfulness hidden from the great assembly.

Ps. 39, ii—"I have proclaimed thy justice in the great assembly; behold, I have not restrained my lips; Lord, thou knowest."

12. Withhold not thy mercies from me, O Lord; * may thy kindness and thy faithfulness guard me always.

13. For evils without number have surrounded me, * my sins have overtaken me, so that I cannot see.

They are more numerous than the hairs of my head, * and my courage has failed me.

Petition

PSALM 39, III

MAY thou, O Lord, be pleased to rescue me; * O Lord, make haste to help me.

Ps. 39, iii—"Let them be turned back and humiliated, who delight in my misfortune."

---

15. Let all be put to confusion and shame, * who seek my life, to snatch it away.

Let them be turned back and humiliated, * who delight in my misfortune.

16. Let them be astounded, covered with confusion, * who say to me: Ha, ha.

17. Let all who seek thee rejoice and be glad in thee, * and let them who love thy help say always: "The Lord is great."

18. But I am wretched and poor; * yet the Lord takes care of me.

Thou art my helper and my deliverer, * my God, do not delay.

Ps. 40—"Happy is he who is considerate of the needy and poor; the Lord will rescue him in the day of trouble."

Prayer of a Sick Man

PSALM 40

Sext

HAPPY is he who is considerate of the needy and poor: * the Lord will rescue him in the day of trouble.

3. The Lord will preserve him and keep him alive, and make him happy upon earth, * and will not deliver him to the will of his enemies.

4. The Lord will support him on his bed of pain: * and in his sickness remove all his weakness.

5. I say: O Lord, be gracious to me; * heal me, for I have sinned against thee.

6. My enemies speak evil of me: * "When shall he die and his name perish?"

7. And if one of them comes to visit me, he does not speak sincerely; * his heart stores up malice, he goes out and then talks.

8. All who hate me whisper together against me; * evil things they plan against me:

9. "A deadly disease has got hold of him," * and "he who lies there shall not rise again."

10. Even my friend, in whom I trusted, * who ate my bread, lifted his heel against me.

11. But thou, O Lord, be gracious to me, and raise me up, * that I may repay them.

12. By this shall I know that thou art pleased with me, * that my enemy shall not triumph over me.

13. But thou wilt sustain me in good health, * and set me in thy sight forever.

14. Blessed be the Lord, the God of Israel, * forever and forever. So be it! So be it!

Homesickness for God's House

PSALM 41, I

AS the deer longs for the streams of water, * so does my soul long for thee, O God.

Ps. 41, i—"As the deer longs for the streams of water, so does my soul long for thee, O God."

---

3. My soul thirsts for God, for the living God: * when shall I come and see the face of God?

4. My tears have become my food day and night, * while they say to me daily: "Where is thy God?"

5. I keep thinking of this and I pour out my very spirit: how I used to walk with the crowd, * and lead them to the house of God, Amid the sounds of joy and praise, * in a festive gathering.

6. Why art thou dejected, O my soul, * and disturbed within me?

Hope in God; for I shall again praise him, * my savior and my God.

Ps. 41, ii—"My bones are being crushed, while my foes taunt me, while they say to me daily: 'Where is thy God?'"

Hope in God

PSALM 41, II

MY soul is depressed within me: * so I will think of thee from the land of the Jordan and Hermon, from the hill of Misar.

8. Deep calls unto deep with the roar of thy waterfalls: * all thy breakers and thy waves have passed over me.

9. By day may the Lord send his mercy, * and at night I will sing to him, I will praise the God of my life.

10. I say to God: my Rock, why hast thou forgotten me? * why must I go about sorrowful, afflicted by my enemy?

11. My bones are being crushed, while my foes taunt me, * while they say to me daily: "Where is thy God?"
12. Why art thou dejected, O my soul, * and disturbed within me?
Hope in God : for I shall again praise him, * my savior, my God.

A Prayer in Time of Affliction Past Mercies Inspire Present Courage

PSALM 43, I

None

WITH our own ears, O God, we have heard, * our fathers have told us
The work thou hast done in their day, * in the days of old.
3. With thy hand thou didst drive out the heathen, and give homes to thy people; * thou didst destroy nations and make room for thy own.
4. For not by their own sword did they take possession of the land, * nor did their own arm give them victory.
It was thy right hand and thy arm * and thy encouraging smile, because thou didst love them.
5. Thou art my king, my God, * who didst grant victories to Jacob.
6. Through thee we have thrust out our enemies, * and in thy name we have trampled upon our opponents.

Ps. 43, i—*"For not by their own sword did they take possession of the land, nor did their own arm give them victory. It was thy right hand and thy arm."*

7. For I have not trusted in my bow, * nor has my sword saved me.

8. But thou hast saved us from our enemies, * and thou didst put to shame those who hate us.

9. In God we gloried at all times, * and to thy name we gave thanks unceasingly.

PSALM 43, II

NOW indeed thou hast cast us off and put us to shame, * and goest not forth, O God, with our armies.

11. Thou hast made us to yield to our enemies, * and they who hate us, plunder us at will.

Ps. 43, ii—"Thou hast made us a reproach to our neighbors, a mockery and a laughing stock to those around us."

---

12. Thou hast handed us over like sheep to be slaughtered, * and hast scattered us among the heathen.

13. Thou hast sold thy people for a mere trifle, * and hast made little profit from their sale.

14. Thou hast made us a reproach to our neighbors, * a mockery and a laughing stock to those around us.

15. Thou hast made us a byword among the heathen, * people shake their heads because of us.

16. My disgrace is always before me, * and shame covers my face,

17. Because of the cry of the scoffer and reviler, * because of the enemy and the revenger.

Appeal for Help

PSALM 43, III

ALL this has come upon us, although we have not forgotten thee, * nor broken thy covenant,

19. Nor has our heart turned aside, * nor has our step strayed from thy path,

20. While thou hast crushed us in the place of affliction, * and hast covered us with darkness.

21. If we had forgotten the name of our God, * and stretched forth our hands to a strange god:

22. Would not God have searched this out? * for he knows the secrets of the heart.

23. But for thy sake we are exposed to death all the time, * we are accounted as sheep for the slaughter.

24. Awake: Why sleepest thou, Lord? * arouse thyself! reject us not forever!

25. Why dost thou hide thy face? * and forget our misery and our oppression?

26. For our soul is brought down to the dust, * our body lies on the ground. Arise to help us, * and rescue us for thy mercy's sake.

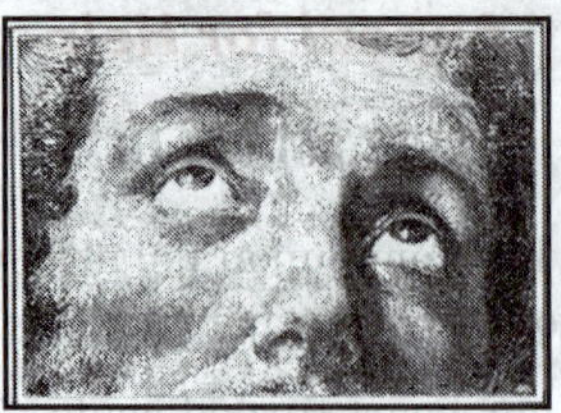

Ps. 122—"I lift up my eyes to thee, who dwellest in heaven."

Appeal to Heaven for Help

PSALM 122

Vespers

I LIFT up my eyes to thee, * who dwellest in heaven.

2. Behold, as the eyes of servants * are on the hands of their masters,

As the eyes of the handmaid * are on the hands of her mistress:

So do our eyes look to the Lord, our God, * until he has mercy on us.

3. Have mercy on us, O Lord, have mercy on us, * for we have been more than filled with scorn;

Our soul is all too full of the mockery of the rich, * of the contempt of the proud.

Temptation Overcome

PSALM 123

IF the Lord had not been on our side, * let Israel now say,
2. If the Lord had not been on our side:
3. when men rose up against us, * then they would have swallowed us alive.
4. When their anger flamed against us, * then the waters would have overwhelmed us;
5. The torrent would have surged over us; * then the swollen waters would have engulfed us.
6. Blessed be the Lord, who did not surrender us * as prey to their teeth.
7. Our soul has been snatched like a bird * from the snare of the fowler.
The snare is broken, * and we are free.
8. Our help is in the name of the Lord, * who made heaven and earth.

Unshaken Trust of the Faithful

PSALM 124

THOSE who trust in the Lord are as Mount Sion, * which is immovable, which abides forever.
2. Mountains surround Jerusalem: * so the Lord surrounds his people, both now and forever.

Ps. 124—"Those who trust in the Lord are as Mount Sion, which is immovable, which abides forever."

Therefore the scepter of the wicked shall not rest * upon the allotted land of the just, Lest the just stretch out * their hands toward evil.

4. Deal kindly, O Lord, with the good * and with the upright of heart.

5. But as for them who go astray on crooked paths, may the Lord drive them away with the evil-doers: * peace be upon Israel!

The Spring of Sorrow and the Harvest of Joy

PSALM 125

WHEN the Lord led back the captives of Sion, * we were like men in a dream.

2. Then was our mouth filled with laughter, * and our tongue with rejoicing.

Then they said among the heathen: "The Lord has done great things for them."

3. The Lord has done great things for us: * we were glad!

4. Change our lot, O Lord, * like the streams in the southland.

5. They who sow in tears, * shall reap in joy.

6. They go forth weeping * who carry seed for sowing:

They shall return rejoicing * bearing their sheaves.

Without Me You Can Do Nothing

PSALM 126

UNLESS the Lord build the house, * they labor in vain who build it.

Unless the Lord protects the city, * the guard keeps watch in vain.

2. In vain do you rise early, * and sit up late,

You who eat hard-earned bread : * for even in the hours of sleep he generously provides for his loved ones.

3. Behold, children are a gift of God, * the fruit of the womb is a reward.

Ps. 126—"Even in the hours of sleep he generously provides for his loved ones."

4. What arrows are in the hands of a warrior, * such are the sons of one's youth.

5. Happy is the man who has filled his quiver with them: * they shall not be put to shame, when they contend with their enemies at the city-gate.

Plea for Protection

PSALM 11

Compline

HELP, O Lord! for faithful men are no more, * faithfulness has died out among men.

3. Everyone tells lies to his neighbor, * they speak with flattering lips and an insincere heart.

Ps. 11—*"Thou, O Lord, wilt keep us and preserve us from this generation forever."*

---

4. May the Lord destroy all deceitful lips, * the boastful tongue,

5. Such as say: "We are heroes with our tongue; our lips are our own: * who is lord over us?"

6. "Because of the misery of the oppressed and the groaning of the poor, I will now arise, says the Lord: * I will bring salvation to him who desires it."

7. The words of the Lord are sincere words, * as silver tried in fire, purged from dross, purified seven times.

8. Thou, O Lord, wilt keep us, * and preserve us from this generation forever.

9. Although the wicked strut around us, * and the vilest of men exalt themselves.

Ps. 12—*"How long, O Lord, wilt thou utterly forget me? . . . Let my heart rejoice because of thy help."*

Confident Prayer in Time of Trial

PSALM 12

HOW long, O Lord, wilt thou utterly forget me? * how long wilt thou hide thy face from me?

3. How long shall I harbor sorrow in my soul, * grief in my heart day after day?

4. How long shall my foe triumph over me? * look on me, answer me, O Lord, my God!

Give light to my eyes, lest I fall asleep in

5. death, * lest my enemy say: "I have vanquished him;"

Let not my enemies rejoice, that I have 6. fallen: * for I have trusted in thy goodness.

Let my heart rejoice because of thy help; * I will sing to the Lord, who has bestowed good things upon me.

Our Inheritance: Eternal Life

PSALM 15

PRESERVE me, O God, for in thee I seek refuge, *

2. I say to the Lord: "Thou art my Lord; I have no good apart from thee."

3. As for the faithful who dwell in his land, * how wonderfully he has fulfilled all my desires.

4. They multiply their sorrows * who follow strange gods.

I will not pour out their drink offerings of blood, * nor will I take their names upon my lips.

5. The Lord is the portion of my inheritance and of my cup: * thou art the one who keepest my allotted portion for me.

6. The lines have fallen for me in pleasant places; * and I am greatly pleased with my inheritance.

7. I bless the Lord who has given me counsel, * because even during the night my heart admonishes me.

Ps. 15—"The Lord is the portion of my inheritance and of my cup."

---

8. I keep the Lord always before me; * since he is at my right, I shall not waver.

9. Therefore my heart rejoices and my soul is glad, * and my body, too, rests secure.

10. For thou wilt not abandon my soul to the abode of the dead, * nor wilt thou let thy holy one see corruption.

11. Thou wilt show me the way of life, the fulness of joy in thy presence, * bliss at thy right hand forever.

Glory be to the Father, and to the Son, and to the Holy Ghost.

As it was in the beginning, is now, and ever shall be, world without end. Amen.

Ps. 44, i—The Messias, Christ the King, in His beauty and splendor, appears as the royal Bridegroom. "Thy throne, O God, is forever and ever."

The Marriage Song of the Redeemer

I Nocturn **PSALM 44, I** Matins

MY heart pours forth a noble theme: I recite my poem to the king; * my tongue is as the pen of a rapid writer.

3. Thou art the fairest among the children of men, grace is poured out upon thy lips: * therefore has God blessed thee forever.

4. Gird thy sword upon thy thigh, O warrior, * gird thyself with thy radiant armour!

5. Go forth victoriously in the cause of faith and justice, * and may thy right hand teach thee wondrous deeds.

6. Thy arrows are sharp, peoples are made subject to thee, * the enemies of the king lose heart.

7. Thy throne, O God, is forever and ever; * the scepter of thy kingdom is a scepter of righteousness.

8. Thou lovest justice and hatest iniquity: therefore God, thy God, has anointed thee, * with the oil of gladness above thy companions.

9. Thy robes are fragrant with myrrh, aloes and cassia; * from ivory palaces the sound of stringed instruments delights thee.

10. The daughters of kings come to meet thee, * the queen stands at thy right hand adorned in gold of Ophir.

The Church: the Bride of Christ

PSALM 44, II

LISTEN, O daughter, consider and incline thy ear, * and forget thy own people and thy father's house.

12. And the king shall greatly desire thy beauty: * he is thy lord; pay homage to him.

13. And the people of Tyre come with gifts; * the princes of the people seek thy favor.

Ps. 44, ii—The Bride symbolizing the Church which Christ has sanctified by His union with it, so that mankind may be reborn into the Divine Family.

14. All resplendent the king's daughter enters; * her robes are embroidered with gold.

15. Clad in a robe of many colors she is led to the king; * in her train virgins, her companions, are brought to thee.

16. They are led in with joy and gladness, * they enter into the palace of the king.

17. In place of thy fathers sons shall be given to thee; * thou shalt make them princes over all the earth.

18. I will remember thy name for all ages; * therefore shall the peoples praise thee forever.

Ps. 45—"The Lord of hosts is with us . . . Who makes wars to cease even unto the ends of the earth."

Confidence in God

PSALM 45

GOD is our refuge and our strength; * he has indeed proved himself a great help in times of distress.

3. Therefore we do not fear, though the earth be overthrown, * and the mountains crash into the midst of the sea.

4. Let its waters roar and rage, * let the mountains be shaken by its violence: The Lord of hosts is with us; * the God of Jacob is our stronghold.

5. The streams of the river gladden the city of God, * the holy dwelling place of the Most High.

6. God is in the midst of it, nor shall it be disturbed; * God will help it at the break of day.

7. Nations were in tumult, kingdoms tottered; * his voice thundered, the earth dissolved:

8. The Lord of hosts is with us; * the God of Jacob is our stronghold.

9. Come, behold the works of the Lord, * what wonders he has done upon earth.

10. Who makes wars to cease even unto the ends of the earth, * he breaks the bows and shatters the spears, and the shields he burns with fire.

11. Desist and know that I am God, * exalted among the nations, exalted on earth.

12. The Lord of hosts is with us; * the God of Jacob is our stronghold.

The Church: the Strong City of God

II Nocturn **PSALM 47** Matins

GREAT is the Lord and highly to be praised, * in the city of our God.

3. His holy mountain, a dazzling height, * it is the joy of the whole world;

Mount Sion, on the northern slope, * is the city of the great King.

4. God in its towers * proved himself a safe defense.

Ps. 47—The Holy City stands impregnable because God reigns there.

---

5. For, behold, the kings assembled, * together they advanced.

6. Scarcely had they beheld it, they were astounded, * they were thrown into confusion and fled.

7. Trembling seized them there, * pain as of a woman in labor,

8. As when the east wind * shatters the ships of Tharsis.

9. As we have heard, so have we seen, * in the city of the Lord of hosts,

In the city of our God: * God makes it firm forever.

10. We recall, O God, thy goodness, * within thy temple.

11. As thy name, O God, so also thy praise * reaches to the ends of the earth.

12. Thy right hand is full of justice: * let Mount Sion rejoice,

Let the cities of Juda be glad * because of thy judgments.

13. Walk through Sion and encircle it, * count its towers.

14. Mark well its defenses, * scan its fortresses,

That you may tell the future generations: *

15. such is God,

Our God forever and always: * he will guide us.

A Lesson for Those Who Envy the Prosperity of the Wicked

PSALM 48, I

HEAR these things, all you peoples; * give ear all you inhabitants of the world,

3. Both low and high, * rich and poor alike.

4. My mouth shall speak wisdom, * and the meditation of my heart shall reveal understanding.

5. I will listen to a proverb, * I will declare my problem to the sound of the lyre.

6. Why should I fear in the days of misfortune, * when the malice of enemies surrounds me,

Ps. 48, i—*"Truly no one can redeem himself, nor pay to God the price of his redemption."*

---

7. Men who trust in their wealth, * and boast of the abundance of their riches?

8. Truly no one can redeem himself, * nor pay to God the price of his redemption:

9. For too costly is the ransom of his life

10. nor would it ever suffice, * that he should live forever and not see the grave.

11. For he sees that wise men die, that the foolish and stupid likewise perish, * and leave their wealth to others.

12. The grave is their home forever, their dwelling for all times, * though lands are named after them.

13. For man does not abide in wealth: * he is like the beasts that perish.

Ps. 48, ii—"Fear not, when a man becomes rich . . . for when he dies, he shall take nothing with him."

Deaths of the Wise and Foolish Differ

PSALM 48, II

THIS is the fate of those who are foolishly self-confident, * and this is the end of those who are pleased with their lot.

15. Like sheep they are herded into hell; * death is their shepherd and the just rule over them.

Quickly their form shall waste away, * hell shall be their home.

16. But God will redeem my soul from hell, * for he will take me to himself.

17. Fear not, when a man becomes rich, * if the wealth of his house be increased:

18. For when he dies, he shall take nothing with him, * and his riches shall not follow him.

19. Though in his lifetime he congratulated himself: * "They shall praise thee, because thou didst well for thyself,"

20. He shall go to the company of his fathers, * who shall not see light forever. Man living in wealth and without understanding * is like the beasts that perish.

True Piety

III Nocturn **PSALM 49, I** Matins

THE Lord God has spoken and summoned the earth * from the rising of the sun to its setting.

2. From Sion, the perfection of beauty, God has shone forth: * our God comes and he is not silent.

3. A consuming fire precedes him, * and a tempest rages around him.

4. He summons the heavens above and the earth, * he is about to judge his people:

5. "Gather my just ones unto me, * who have ratified my covenant with sacrifice."

6. And the heavens proclaim his justice, * for God himself is judge.

Ps. 49, i—Interior holiness must accompany external worship, for all nature belongs to God, its Creator.

---

7. "Listen, my people, and I will speak, Israel, and I will testify against thee: * I am God, thy God.

8. Not for thy sacrifices do I reprove thee, * indeed thy burnt-offerings are always before me.

9. I will take no bullock from thy house, * nor he-goats from thy flocks:

10. For all the beasts of the forest are mine, * the countless cattle upon my mountains.

11. I know all the birds of the air, * and whatever moves in the field, is known to me.

12. If I were hungry, I would not tell thee: * for the world is mine and the fulness thereof.

13. Shall I eat the flesh of bulls, * or drink the blood of he-goats?

14. Offer to God a sacrifice of thanksgiving, * and pay thy vows to the Most High.

15. And call upon me in the day of trouble: * I will deliver thee and thou shalt honor me."

God Rebukes Lip-Service Without Deeds

PSALM 49, II

BUT to the sinner God says: "Why dost thou recite my precepts, * and profess my covenant with thy mouth?

17. Thou who hatest discipline * and hast cast my words behind thee?

18. When thou didst see a thief, thou didst run along with him, * and with adulterers thou didst make common cause.

19. Thou didst open thy mouth to evil, * and thy tongue contrived deceit.

Ps.49, ii—*To the sinner God says: "Consider this, you who forget God, lest I snatch you away and there be none to save you."*

---

20. Thou didst sit and speak against thy brother, * and slander thy own mother's son.

21. These things thou hast done and shall I be silent? didst thou think that I was like thee? * I will reprove thee and lay these things before thy eyes.

22. Consider this, you who forget God, * lest I snatch you away and there be none to save you.

23. He who offers a sacrifice of thanksgiving honors me, * and to him who walks in the right path I will show the salvation of God.

Ps. 50—"Have mercy on me, O God . . . My sin is always before me."

An Act of Contrition

PSALM 50

HAVE mercy on me, O God, according to thy mercy; * according to thy great clemency blot out my iniquity.

4. Wash me completely from my guilt, * and cleanse me from my sin.

5. For I acknowledge my iniquity, * and my sin is always before me.

6. Against thee only have I sinned, * and I have done what is evil in thy sight,

This I confess that thou mayest be known to be just in thy sentence, * right in thy judgment.

7. Behold, I was born in guilt, * and my mother conceived me in sin.

8. Behold, thou dost delight in sincerity of heart, * and teachest me wisdom in the depths of my soul.

9. Sprinkle me with hyssop, that I may be cleansed; * wash me, that I may become whiter than snow.

10. Let me hear sounds of joy and gladness, * let the bones which thou hast crushed rejoice.

11. Turn away thy face from my sins, * and blot out all my guilt.

12. Create a clean heart for me, O God, * and renew in me a steadfast spirit.

13. Cast me not off from thy presence, * and take not thy holy spirit from me.

14. Restore to me the joy of thy salvation, * and strengthen me with a generous spirit.

15. I will teach the unjust thy ways, * and sinners shall be converted to thee.

16. Deliver me from blood-guilt, O God, God my savior: * let my tongue rejoice because of thy justice.

17. O Lord, open thou my lips, * and my mouth shall declare thy praise.

18. For thou dost not delight in sacrifice; * and a burnt-offering thou wouldst not accept, if I offered it.

19. My sacrifice, O God, is a contrite spirit, * a contrite and humbled heart, O God, thou wilt not despise.

20. In thy goodness, O Lord, deal kindly with Sion, * that thou mayest rebuild the walls of Jerusalem.

Then wilt thou accept lawful sacrifices, oblations and burnt-offerings, * then will they offer bullocks on thy altar.

The Lord of the World

PSALM 96

Lauds

THE Lord is king: let the earth rejoice, * let the many islands be glad.

2. Clouds and darkness are round about him, * justice and right are the foundation of his throne.

3. A fire goes before him, * and devours his enemies round about.

4. His lightnings illumine the world; * the earth sees and trembles.

5. The mountains melt like wax before the Lord, * before the Lord of all the earth.

6. The heavens declare his justice; * and all peoples behold his glory.

Ps. 96—"Light shines forth for the just one."

7. Confounded are all who worship graven images and boast of their idols; * all the gods fall prostrate before him.

8. Sion hears and rejoices, and the cities of Juda are glad, * because of thy judgments, O Lord.

9. For thou, O Lord, art sovereign over all the earth, * supremely exalted above all the gods.

10. The Lord loves those who hate evil, he preserves the lives of his faithful ones, * he saves them from the hand of the wicked.

11. Light shines forth for the just one, * and joy for the upright of heart.

12. Rejoice in the Lord, you just, * and praise his holy name.

Ps. 64—*"Thou has visited the land and watered it, thou hast greatly enriched it."*

A Prayer of Thanksgiving for Benefits Received

PSALM 64

TO thee, O God, is due a song of praise in Sion, * let a vow be paid to thee,

3. who hearest prayers.

4. To thee every mortal comes * because of his iniquities.

Our sins are heavy upon us: * thou forgivest them.

5. Happy the man whom thou dost choose and take * to dwell in thy courts.

May we be filled with the good things of thy house, * with the holiness of thy temple.

6. By wondrous signs thou dost answer us with justice, * O God, our savior,

Thou, the hope of all the world * and of distant seas,

7. Thou who in thy strength dost establish mountains, * thou, girt with power,

8. Who stillest the roaring of the sea, * the roaring of its waves and the tumult of the nations:

9. And the most distant inhabitants of the earth are awed at thy signs; * thou fillest with joy the distant lands of East and West.

10. Thou hast visited the land and watered it, * thou hast greatly enriched it.

The river of God is filled with water, thou hast prepared their corn; * for so thou hast prepared the land:

11. Thou hast watered its furrows, * thou hast leveled its clods,

Thou hast softened it with rains, * thou hast blessed its growth.

12. Thou hast crowned the year with thy goodness, * and thy tracks drip with fertility.

13. The pastures of the wilderness drip with fertility, * and the hills are girded with gladness.

14. The meadows are clothed with flocks, and the valleys are covered with corn: * they shout for joy and sing.

Ps. 100—The Just Ruler "cutting off from the city of the Lord every evildoer."

The Just Ruler

PSALM 100

I WILL sing of kindness and justice; * to thee, O Lord, will I sing praises.

2. I will advance in the way of perfection: * when wilt thou come to me?

I will walk in the simplicity of my heart * within my own home.

3. I will put before my eyes * no base thing;

I hate the evil-doer: * he shall not remain close to me.

4. The perverse heart shall be far from me; * I want to know nothing of evil.

5. The man who secretly slanders his neighbor: * him will I destroy.

The man of haughty eyes and proud heart: * him I will not tolerate.

6. My eyes are upon the faithful of the land, * that they may dwell with me.

He who walks in the way of perfection, * he shall serve me.

7. He who practises deceit * shall have no place in my house.

He who tells lies shall not remain * in my presence.

8. Day by day I will destroy * all the sinners of the land,

Cutting off from the city of the Lord * every evil-doer.

CANTICLE OF JUDITH

I WILL sing a hymn to the Lord, * I will sing a new hymn to my God.

16. O Lord, thou art great and glorious, * thou art wonderful in power and not to be surpassed.

17. Let every creature of thine serve thee, * for thou didst speak, and they were made,

Thou didst send forth thy spirit, and they were created, * nor does any one resist thy voice.

Canticle of Judith—Judith after freeing her city by beheading Holofernes, the general of the Assyrian army, sings a hymn of thanksgiving.

---

18. For the mountains are moved from their foundations with the waters; * the rocks melt like wax before thee.

19. But to them who fear thee, * thou art gracious,

Because every sacrifice having a sweet odor is small, * and very small to thee is all the fat of a burnt-offering;

But he who fears the Lord, * shall be great in every way.

20. Woe to the nations that rise up against my people: * the Lord of hosts will take revenge on them in the day of judgment. He will send fire and worms into their flesh, * and they shall weep in sorrow forever.

Ps. 145—"Put not your trust in princes, in man, in whom there is no help . . . Happy the man . . . whose hope is in the Lord, his God."

Prayer Against Over-Confidence in Self

PSALM 145

PRAISE the Lord, O my soul; I will praise the Lord my life long; * I will sing praises to my God as long as I live.

3. Put not your trust in princes, * in man, in whom there is no help.

4. When his spirit departs, he returns to dust; * then all his plans shall perish.

5. Happy the man whose helper is the God of Jacob, * whose hope is in the Lord, his God,

6. Who made heaven and earth, * the sea, and all that is therein,

7. Who remains faithful forever, who renders justice to the oppressed, * gives bread to the hungry.

8. The Lord releases the captives, * the Lord opens the eyes of the blind.

The Lord raises up those who are bowed down, * the Lord loves the just.

9. The Lord watches over strangers, he supports the orphan and the widow, * but the way of sinners he thwarts.

10. The Lord will reign forever, * thy God, O Sion, throughout the ages.

Prayer Before Holy Communion

PSALM 25

Prime

DO me justice, O Lord, for I have walked in my innocence, * and trusting in the Lord, I have not wavered.

2. Subject me to scrutiny, O Lord, and try me; * test my feelings and my heart.

3. For thy kindness is before my eyes, * and I walk according to thy truth.

4. I do not sit with unjust men, * nor do I associate with deceivers.

5. I hate the company of evil-doers * and I sit not down with the wicked.

Ps. 25—*"O Lord, I love the house where thou dwellest and the dwelling place of thy glory."*

---

6. I wash my hands in innocence * and I walk around thy altar, O Lord,

7. That I may proclaim aloud thy praise, * and recount all thy wondrous deeds.

8. O Lord, I love the house where thou dwellest * and the dwelling place of thy glory.

9. Snatch not my soul away with sinners * nor my life with murderers,

10. On whose hands is crime, * and whose right hand is full of bribes.

11. But I walk in my innocence: * deliver me and be gracious to me.

12. My foot stands on level ground, * in the assemblies I will bless the Lord.

Ps. 51—*"Behold the man who made not God his refuge, but trusted in the abundance of his riches."*

The Evil of Calumny

PSALM 51

WHY do you boast of evil, * O man mighty in crime?

4. You are forever plotting ruin, * your tongue is like a sharp razor, you mischief maker.

5. You love evil rather than good, * lying rather than righteous speech.

6. You love all pernicious speech, * O deceitful tongue!

7. Therefore, God will destroy you, * and remove you forever,
He will snatch you from your dwelling * and uproot you from the land of the living.

8. The just shall see and fear * and shall laugh at him, saying:

9. "Behold the man who made not God * his refuge,

But trusted in the abundance of his riches, * and grew powerful by his crimes."

10. But I am like a green olive-tree in the house of God; * I put my trust in the goodness of God forever.

11. I will give thee thanks forever, because thou hast done *this* and I will proclaim thy name, * for it is good, in the presence of thy faithful.

Prayer for Understanding

PSALM 52

THE fool says in his heart: * "There is no God." They are corrupt, they have done abominable things; * there is none who does good.

3. God looks down from heaven upon men, * to see if there be one who is wise and seeks God.

4. All have gone astray together, all are perverted; * there is none who does good, not even one.

5. Will not evildoers return to their senses, * who devour my people as they eat bread, and call not upon God?

Ps. 52—If the wicked do not return to their senses, they shall not escape divine punishment.

6. There did they tremble with fear, * where there was no reason to fear,

For God scattered the bones of those who besieged you; * they were put to shame, because God has rejected them.

7. Oh, may the deliverance of Israel come forth from Sion! When God shall restore the fortune of his people, * Jacob shall rejoice, Israel shall be glad.

A Cry for Help in Time of Need

PSALM 53

Terce

O GOD, save me by thy name, * and defend my cause by thy might.

Ps. 53—*"O God, hear my prayer . . . for proud men have risen against me."*

---

4. O God, hear my prayer; * give heed to the words of my mouth.

5. For proud men have risen against me, and violent men have sought my life; * they have not set God before them.

6. Behold, God helps me, * the Lord is the support of my life.

7. Make the evil recoil upon my enemies * and according to thy faithfulness destroy them.

8. Gladly will I sacrifice to thee, * I will praise thy name, O Lord, for it is good.

9. For he has delivered me from all adversity, * and my eye has seen my enemies put to shame.

Ps. 54, i—"Oh that I had wings like a dove, I would fly away and be at rest."

A Prayer to Overcome the Fear of Death

PSALM 54, I

O GOD, hear my prayer, and hide not thyself from my pleading, * listen to me and answer me.

3. In my anguish I am bewildered, * and

4. troubled by the voice of the foe, the cry of the sinner.

For they bring evils upon me * and with fury they attack me.

5. My heart is troubled within me, * and the terror of death falls upon me.

6. Fear and trembling come upon me, * and horror overwhelms me.

7. And I say: Oh that I had wings like a dove, * I would fly away and be at rest;
8. Behold, I would go far away, * I would live in the wilderness.
9. Swiftly would I seek refuge for myself * from the whirlwind and the storm.
10. Destroy them, O Lord, divide their tongues; * for I see violence and discord in the city.
11. Day and night they go about on its walls, * and wickedness and oppression are in its midst.
12. Treachery is within it, * and violence and deceit depart not from its streets.
13. If an enemy had insulted me, * truly I could have borne it;
If he who hates me, had risen against me, * I could have hidden myself from him.
14. But it was thou, my comrade, * my intimate friend,
15. With whom I had sweet companionship, * in the house of God we walked with the festive throng.

Confidence in God

PSALM 54, II

MAY death overtake them, may they go down alive to hell, * for there is wickedness in their dwellings, in their midst.

Ps. 54, ii—"But I will cry aloud to God, and the Lord will save me."

---

17. But I will cry aloud to God, * and the Lord will save me.

18. Evening, morning and noon will I lament and sigh, * and he will hear my voice.

19. He will deliver me safely from those who attack me: * for many are against me.

20. God, who reigns from eternity, will hear me and humble them; * for they do not improve, nor do they fear God.

21. Everyone strikes out against his intimate friends, * he violates his pact.

22. Smoother than butter is his face, * but war is in his heart.

His words are softer than oil, * but they are drawn swords.

23. Cast thy care upon the Lord, and he will sustain thee: * he will never permit the just to waver.

24. And thou, O God, wilt bring them down * to the pit of ruin;

Bloody and deceitful men shall not live out half their days, * but I put my trust in thee, O Lord.

Prayer in Time of Temptation

PSALM 55

Sext

HAVE mercy on me, O God, for men do trample upon me. * they oppress and attack me without ceasing.

3. My foes are forever treading on me, * for many fight against me.

4. O Most High,' in the day when fear comes upon me, * I will trust in thee.

5. In God, whose promise I praise, in God I put my trust, I will not fear: * what can man do to me?

6. All day long they disparage me, * all their thoughts are against me, unto harm.

7. They gather together, they lie in wait, they watch my footsteps, * seeking my life.

8. Repay them for the evil, * in wrath, O God, cast down the peoples.

Ps. 55—*"In God I put my trust, I will not fear: what can man do to me?"*

---

9. Thou hast kept account of the ways of my exile; my tears are kept in thy waterskin : * are they not recorded in thy book?

10. Then shall my enemies turn back, whenever I call upon thee; * by this I know well that God is on my side.

11. In God, whose promise I praise,

12. in God I put my trust, I will not fear: * what can man do to me?

13. I am held to the vows, O God, which I made to thee, * I will fulfill the thank-offerings to thee,

14. For thou hast delivered my life from death, and my feet from stumbling, * so that I may walk before God in the light of the living.

Ps. 56—"In the shadow of thy wings I seek refuge, till the disaster be past."

A Prayer for Mercy

PSALM 56

HAVE mercy on me, O God, have mercy on me, * for in thee my soul takes refuge,

And in the shadow of thy wings I seek refuge, * till the disaster be past.

3. I cry to God Most High, * to God, my benefactor.

4. May he send help from heaven to save me, may he bring disgrace upon those who persecute me; * may God send his grace and faithfulness.

5. I lie down in the midst of lions, * that greedily devour men.

Their teeth are spears and arrows, * and their tongue is a sharp sword.

6. Be thou exalted, O God, above the heavens; * may thy glory be over all the earth.

7. They have laid a snare for my feet: * and bowed down my soul;

They dug a pit before me: * may they fall into it.

8. My heart is steadfast, O God, my heart is steadfast; * I will chant and sing praises.

9. Awake, O my soul; awake harp and lyre! * I will awaken the dawn.

10. I will praise thee, O Lord, among the peoples; * I will sing praises to thee among the nations,

11. For thy goodness is great even unto the heavens, * and thy faithfulness unto the clouds.

12. Be thou exalted, O God, above the heavens; * may thy glory be over all the earth!

Unjust Rulers

PSALM 57

DO you really administer justice, you mighty ones? * do you judge rightly, you men?

3. Rather do you plan evil in your heart, * and your hands deal out injustice in the land.

4. The wicked go astray even from their mother's womb, * even from birth these liars have erred.

5. Their poison is like the poison of a serpent, * like that of a deaf adder that stops its ears,

6. Lest it hear the voice of charmers, * of the skilful binder of spells.

7. O God, break their teeth in their mouth; * break the jaw-teeth of the lions, O Lord.

8. Let them vanish like the waters that flow away; * if they shoot their arrows, let them become blunted.

9. Let them pass like the snail that wastes away, * like a woman's untimely birth that sees not the sun.

10. Before your kettles can feel the burning thorn-bush, * may the hot blast of the whirlwind carry it away, while it is yet green.

11. The just man shall rejoice when he sees vengeance, * he shall wash his feet in the blood of the wicked.

12. And men shall say: Truly there is a reward for the just man, * truly there is a God who judges on earth.

Ps. 58, i—*"Deliver me from my enemies, O my God . . . For, behold, they lie in wait for my life."*

God Is Our Strength

PSALM 58, I

None

DELIVER me from my enemies, O my God, * protect me from my aggressors.

3. Deliver me from malefactors, * and save me from blood-thirsty men.

4. For, behold, they lie in wait for my life, * powerful men plot against me.

There is neither crime nor sin in me,

5. O Lord: * without fault of mine they run forward and attack me.

6. Awake, come to meet me, and see; * for thou, O Lord of hosts, art the God of Israel.

Rise up, chastise all the nations, * have no pity upon any of the traitors.

7. They return at evening, they howl like dogs, * and prowl about the city;

8. Behold, they boast with their mouth; insults are on their lips: * "For who hears" they say.

9. But thou, O Lord, dost laugh at them, * thou dost deride all the nations.

10. O my strength, to thee will I turn, for

11. thou, O God, art my defense, * my God, my mercy.

PSALM 58, II

MAY God come to my help, * may he let me gloat over my enemies.

12. Slay them, O God, lest they seduce my people, * upset them by thy power and lay them low, O Lord, my shield.

13. Every word of their lips is a sin of their mouth, * let them be caught in their pride and because of the curses and lies which they utter.

Ps. 58, ii—*David escapes from his enemies.*

14. Destroy them in wrath, destroy them, so that they be no more, * so that it be known that God reigns over Jacob and unto the ends of the earth.

15. They return at evening, they howl like dogs, * and prowl about the city;

16. They wander about looking for food; * they howl, if they are not filled.

17. But I will sing of thy strength, * and in the morning I will rejoice in thy goodness,

For thou hast become my defense, * and a refuge in the day of my distress.

18. O my strength, to thee will I sing praise, for thou, O God, art my defense, * my God, my mercy.

Ps. 59—"Wilt thou not march forth once again, O God, with our armies?"

Strength in Temptation

PSALM 59

O GOD thou hast rejected us, thou hast shattered our battle lines, * thou hast been angry: restore us.

4. Thou hast shaken the earth, thou hast torn it apart; * heal its breaches: for it quakes.

5. Thou hast laid hardships upon thy people; * thou hast made us to drink of a heady wine.

6. Thou hast raised a banner for those who fear thee, * that they might flee from the bow;

7. That thy beloved might be delivered, * help with thy right hand, and answer us.

8. God spoke in his sanctuary: * "I will rejoice and I will divide Sichem, and I will measure out the valley of Succoth.

9. Mine is the land of Galaad and mine the land of Manasses, * and Ephraim is the defense of my head, Juda my scepter.

10. Moab is my wash-basin; upon Edom I will cast my sandal, * over Philistia I will shout in triumph.

11. Who will bring me into the fortified city? * who will lead me into Edom? *

12. Is it not thou, O God, who hast rejected us, * and wilt thou not march forth once again, O God, with our armies?

13. Give us help against the foe, * for man's help is futile.

14. Through God we shall do valiantly, * and he will crush our enemies.

The Blessing of a Religious Home-Life

PSALM 127

Vespers

HAPPY is everyone who fears the Lord, * and walks in his ways!

Ps. 127—*"For you shall eat of the toil of your hands, you shall be happy and it shall be well with you . . . Behold, thus is the man blessed, who fears the Lord."*

---

2. For you shall eat of the toil of your hands, * you shall be happy and it shall be well with you.

3. Your wife shall be as a fruitful vine * in the interior of your house,

Your children shall be as olive plants * around your table.

4. Behold, thus is the man blessed, * who fears the Lord!

5. May the Lord bless you from Sion, * that you may see the welfare of Jerusalem all the days of your life;

6. That you may see your children's children: * peace be upon Israel!

Oppressed but Never Conquered

PSALM 128

GREATLY have they oppressed me from my youth, * let Israel now say:

2. Greatly have they oppressed me from my youth, * but they have not conquered me.

3. The plowmen plowed upon my back, * they made their furrows long.

4. But the just Lord * has cut the cords of the wicked.

5. Let them be put to shame and fall back * all who hate Sion.

6. Let them be as the grass on the housetops, * which withers before it is plucked up;

7. Wherewith the reaper fills not his hand, * nor the binder of sheaves his bosom.

8. Nor do they who pass by, say: "The blessing of the Lord be upon you!" * "we bless you in the name of the Lord."

Ps. 129—"Out of the depths I cry to thee, O Lord,"

PSALM 129

OUT of the depths I cry to thee, O Lord, * O Lord, hear my voice!

2. Let thy ears be attentive * to the voice of my supplication.

3. If thou shouldst remember sins, O Lord, * O Lord, who could bear it?

4. But with thee is forgiveness, * that thou mayest be served with reverence.

5. I hope in the Lord, * my soul hopes in his word;
6. My soul waits for the Lord, * more than watchmen for the dawn.
More than watchmen for the dawn, *
7. let Israel wait for the Lord,
For with the Lord is mercy * and with him plenteous redemption:

8. And he shall redeem Israel * from all its sins.

Resignation to the Will of God

PSALM 130

O LORD, my heart is not proud, * nor are my eyes haughty,

Neither do I deal in great affairs * nor in things too lofty for me.

2. Truly I have calmed and quieted * my soul,

As a little child on its mother's lap: * as a little child, so is my soul within me.

3. O Israel, hope in the Lord, * both now and forever.

Devotion to the Church and Holy Eucharist

PSALM 131

TO please David, O Lord, * remember all his anxious care:

2. How he swore to the Lord, * vowed to the Mighty One of Jacob:

3. "I will not enter the house where I dwell, * nor mount the bed where I lie,

4. I will not grant sleep to my eyes, * nor rest to my eyelids,

5. Until I find a place for the Lord, * a dwelling for the Mighty One of Jacob."

6. Behold, we have heard of it in Ephrata; * we have found it in the fields of Jaar.

7. Let us enter his dwelling place, * let us worship at his footstool.

8. Arise, O Lord, to thy resting-place, * thou and thy majestic ark.

9. Let thy priests be clothed with justice, * and thy faithful ones shout with joy.

10. For the sake of David, thy servant, * refuse not the plea of thy anointed.

11. The Lord has sworn to David * a lasting promise from which he will not depart: "The offspring of thy race * I will set upon thy throne.

12. If thy children will keep my pact, * and the precepts which I shall teach them, Their sons also forever * shall sit upon thy throne."

13. For the Lord has chosen Sion, * he has desired it for his dwelling place:

14. "This is my resting-place forever, * here will I dwell, for I have desired it.

15. I will abundantly bless its food stock, * I will satiate its poor with bread.

16. Its priests will I clothe with salvation, * and its faithful ones shall shout with joy.

17. There will I exalt the power of David, * I will prepare a lamp for my anointed.

18. His enemies will I clothe with shame, * but upon him my crown shall shine."

Ps. 33, i—"Taste and see how good the Lord is; happy the man who takes refuge in him."

Praise the Lord, Our Only Refuge

PSALM 33, I

Compline

I WILL bless the Lord at all times: * his praise shall be ever in my mouth.

3. Let my soul glory in the Lord: * let the humble hear and rejoice.

4. Glorify the Lord with me; * and let us together exalt his name.

5. I sought the Lord, and he answered me; * and he delivered me from all my fears.

6. Look unto him, that you may be filled with joy, * and your face be not covered with shame.

7. Behold, the poor man cried, and the Lord heard, * and helped him out of all his troubles.

8. The angel of the Lord encamps round those who fear him, * and he rescues them.

9. Taste and see how good the Lord is; * happy the man who takes refuge in him.

10. Fear the Lord, you his faithful ones, * for nothing is wanting to those who fear him.

11. The powerful have become poor and hungry; * but they who seek the Lord shall not lack any good thing.

Blessings of the Faithful Soul

PSALM 33, II

COME, children, listen to me; * I will teach you the fear of the Lord.

13. Who is the man who loves life, * desires length of days to enjoy prosperity?

14. Keep thy tongue from evil, * and thy lips from deceitful words.

15. Depart from evil and do good; * seek peace and pursue it.

16. The eyes of the Lord are upon the just, * his ears open to their cry.

17. The face of the Lord is against evildoers, * to destroy the remembrance of them from the earth.

Ps. 33, ii—"Come children, listen to me; I will teach you the fear of the Lord."

---

18. The just cried and the Lord answered them; * and delivered them from all their troubles.

19. The Lord is close to the brokenhearted, * and saves those of contrite spirit.

20. Many are the trials of the just man; * but the Lord delivers him from all.

21. He guards all his bones: * not one of them shall be broken.

22. Evil shall slay the wicked, * and they who hate the just shall be punished.

23. The Lord delivers the souls of his servants, * and whoever flees to him for refuge shall not be punished.

Ps. 60—"O God . . . listen to my prayer. From the ends of the earth I cry to thee."

God Is Our Strong Defense

PSALM 60

O GOD, hear my cry, * listen to my prayer.
3. From the ends of the earth I cry to thee, *
for my heart is faint.

Thou wilt set me high upon a rock, thou wilt

4. give me rest, * for thou art my refuge, a tower of strength against the enemy.

5. May I dwell in thy tabernacle forever, * may I find refuge in the shelter of thy wings!

6. For thou, O God, hast heard my vows; * thou hast given me the inheritance of those who reverence thy name.

7. Do thou add days to the days of the king, * may his years equal many generations;

8. May he reign before God forever; * send grace and faithfulness to guard him.

9. So will I sing praise to thy name forever, * and daily pay my vows.

Glory be to the Father, and to the Son and to the Holy Ghost . . .

Ps. 61—"In God alone be at rest, O my soul, for my hope comes from him."

Trust in God

I Nocturn **PSALM 61** Matins

IN God alone is my soul at rest, * from him comes my salvation.

3. He alone is my rock and my salvation, * my defense: in no wise shall I waver.

4. How long will you rush upon a man, to overthrow him, all of you * like a leaning wall of a house, or a tottering wall of a city.

5. Truly, they plot to hurl me from my high place, * they delight in lies;

They bless with their mouth, * and they curse in their heart.

6. In God alone be at rest, O my soul, * for my hope comes from him.

7. He alone is my rock and my salvation, * my defense: I shall not waver.

8. God alone possesses my salvation and my glory, * the rock of my strength: my refuge is in God.

9. Trust in him at all times, O people; pour out your hearts before him: * God is our refuge!

10. The children of the lowly are but a breath, * the children of the lofty are false. In the scales they rise high, * all together they are lighter than a breath.

11. Rely not on violence, and glory not vainly in plunder; * if wealth increase, set not your heart upon it.

12. Once God spoke; these two things have I heard: "power belongs to God, and to thee, O Lord, mercy; * for thou dost render to every man according to his work."

Gratitude for Deliverance

PSALM 65, I

SHOUT joyfully to God, all the earth, chant the glory of his name, * render to him noble praise.

3. Say to God: how wondrous are thy works! * because of thy great power thy enemies respect thee.

Ps. 65, i—"Let all the earth worship thee."

4. Let all the earth worship thee and sing praise to thee, * sing praise to thy name.

5. Come and see the works of God: * the wondrous works he wrought among men!

6. He changed the sea into dry land; they crossed the river on foot: * therefore let us rejoice in him!

7. He rules by his might forever; his eyes watch the nations: * let not the rebellious exalt themselves.

8. Bless our God, O nations, * and let his praise resound.

9. Who has kept us among the living, * and has not allowed our foot to stumble.

10. For thou hast tested us, O God; * thou hast tried us by fire, as silver is tried;

11. Thou hast led us into a snare; * thou hast laid a heavy burden on our backs;

12. Thou hast made men to ride over our heads; we went through fire and water: * but thou gavest us relief.

Personal Gratitude

PSALM 65, II

I WILL enter thy house with burnt-offerings, * I will pay thee my vows,

14. Which my lips uttered and my mouth promised, * when I was in distress.

15. I will offer thee burnt-offerings of fat sheep with the fat of rams: * I will sacrifice bullocks and goats.

16. Come, hear, all you who fear God, and I will tell you, * what great things he has done for me!

17. I cried to him with my mouth, * and I praised him with my tongue.

18. If I had intended evil in my heart, * the Lord would not have answered.

19. But God has answered: * he gave heed to my prayer.

20. Blessed be God, who did not reject my prayer, * nor withdraw his mercy from me.

Ps. 67, i—"O God, when thou didst go forth before thy people, when thou didst march through the wilderness, the earth quaked . . . Sinai trembled before God."

A Chant of Triumph

PSALM 67, I

II Nocturn

GOD arises, his foes are scattered, * and they who hate him flee from his presence.

3. As smoke is driven away, so are they driven away, as wax melts before the fire, * so sinners perish before God.

4. But the just are glad, they rejoice in the sight of God, * and they rejoice exceedingly.

5. Sing to God, sing praises to his name; * prepare the way for him who rides through the desert,

Whose name is the Lord, * and rejoice before him.

6. The father of orphans and the guardian of widows * God is in his holy dwelling place.

7. God provides a home for the abandoned, he leads captives forth to prosperity: * only the rebellious dwell in a parched land.

8. O God, when thou didst go forth before thy people, * when thou didst march through the wilderness,

9. The earth quaked, rain also fell from the heavens before God, * Sinai trembled before God, the God of Israel.

10. A copious rain didst thou pour upon thy inheritance, O God, * and when it was parched, thou didst refresh it.

11. Thy flock dwelt therein, * in thy goodness, O God, thou didst prepare it for the poor.

The Lord Enthroned on Sion

PSALM 67, II

THE Lord utters the word; * great is the throng bringing good news:

13. "Kings of armies flee, they flee; * and those at home divide the spoil

14. While you were lingering among the sheepfolds, the wings of the dove were shining with silver, * and its pinions with glittering gold.

15. While the Almighty was scattering kings therein, * snow fell on Salmon!"

16. Lofty mountains are the mountains of Basan, * the mountains of Basan are rugged:

17. Rugged mountains, why look you enviously, at the mountain whereon God desired to dwell, * nay more whereon the Lord will dwell forever?

18. Many are the chariots of God, thousands upon thousands: * the Lord came from Sinai into the sanctuary.

19. Thou hast ascended on high, thou hast brought captives, thou hast received men as gifts, * even those who refuse to dwell with the Lord God.

20. Blessed be the Lord day by day: * God, our salvation, bears our burdens!

21. Our God is a God of deliverance, * and the Lord God gives escape from death.

22. Truly, God crushes the heads of his foes, * the hairy head of him who walks in his sins.

23. The Lord said: "I will bring them back from Basan, * I will bring them back from the depths of the sea,

24. That thou mayest dip thy foot in blood, * that the tongues of thy dogs may have their share of the enemies."

Ps. 67, iii—"They see thy procession, O God, the procession of my God, my king, to the sanctuary."

A Procession of Thanksgiving

PSALM 67, III

THEY see thy procession, O God, * the procession of my God, my king, to the sanctuary:

26. The singers lead, the minstrels follow, * in their midst maidens play timbrels.

27. "Bless God in festive gatherings, * the Lord, you who are born of Israel."

28. There is Benjamin, the youngest, at their head, the princes of Juda with their throngs, * the princes of Zabulon, the princes of Nephtali.

29. Display thy power, O God, * thy power, O God, who hast labored for us!

30. Because of thy temple which is in Jerusalem, * let kings offer gifts to thee!

31. Rebuke the wild beast of the reeds, * the herd of bulls with the calves of the peoples,
Let them prostrate themselves with pieces of silver: * scatter the nations that delight in wars.
32. Let the ambassadors come from Egypt, * let Ethiopia stretch out its hands to God.
33. O kingdoms of the earth, sing to God,
34. sing praises to the Lord, * who rides through the heavens, the heavens of old! Behold, he sends forth his voice,
35. a mighty voice: * "Acknowledge the might of God!"
His majesty is over Israel, * and his power in the clouds.
36. Awesome is God from his holy place, the God of Israel; he gives power and strength to his people: * Blessed be God!

Prayer in Time of Suffering

PSALM 68, I

III Nocturn

SAVE me, O God, * for the waters have mounted to my neck.
3. I am sunk in deep mire, * where there is no foothold;
I have come into deep waters, * and the flood overwhelms me.

Ps. 68, i—"Save me, O God, for the waters have mounted to my neck."

---

4. I am worn out by my crying, * my throat has become hoarse;
My eyes fail, * while I wait for my God.
5. More numerous than the hairs of my head, * are they who hate me without cause,
Above my strength are they who oppose me unjustly: * must I restore what I have not stolen?
6. O God, thou knowest my foolishness, * and my faults are not hidden from thee.
7. Let not those who hope in thee be put to shame through me, * O Lord, Lord of hosts.
Let not those who seek thee be brought to disgrace through me, * O God of Israel.
8. Because I have borne reproach for thy sake, * shame has covered my face.
9. I have become a stranger to my brothers, * and an alien to my mother's sons.

10. For I am consumed with zeal for thy house, * and the reproaches of those who reproach thee have fallen on me.

11. I afflicted myself by fasting, * and it became a reproach to me.

12. I put on sack cloth as my garment, * and I became a joke to them.

13. They who sit at the gate gossip about me * and wine-drinkers revile me.

Plea for Help

PSALM 68, II

TO thee, O Lord, my prayer is directed, * at an acceptable time, O God;

In thy great goodness answer me, * according to thy faithful help.

15. Rescue me from the mire, lest I sink, deliver me from those who hate me, * and from the deep waters.

16. Let not the floods overwhelm me, let not the deep swallow me up, * let not the pit close its mouth upon me!

17. Answer me, O Lord, for thy mercy is gracious; * in thy great mercy look upon me,

Ps. 68, ii—"And they put gall into my food, and in my thirst they gave me vinegar to drink."

18. And do not hide thy face from thy servant; * for I am in trouble, answer me quickly.

19. Draw near to me, redeem me; * because of my enemies release me.

20. Thou knowest my reproach, my shame and my disgrace; * my foes are all before thee.

21. Reproach has broken my heart and I have become weak, and I looked for one to pity me, but there was none, * and for someone to comfort me, but I found none.

22. And they put gall into my food, * and in my thirst they gave me vinegar to drink.

23. May their table become a snare for them, * and a trap for their friends.

24. Let their eyes be darkened, that they may not see, * and make their loins tremble constantly.

25. Pour out thy anger upon them, * and may the fury of thy wrath overtake them.

26. May their dwelling be laid waste, * and may there be none to dwell in their tents.

27. For they persecute him whom thou hast smitten, * and they have increased the pain of him whom thou hast wounded.

28. Add guilt to their guilt, * and may they not be declared just before thee.

29. May they be blotted out of the book of the living, * and not be recorded among the just.

Confident of Deliverance

PSALM 68, III

BUT I am wretched and in pain, * may thy help, O God, protect me.

31. I will praise the name of God in song, * and I will glorify him with thanksgiving.

32. And this will please God more than an ox, * more than a bullock with horns and hoofs.

33. See, O you humble people, and rejoice, * let your heart be revived, you who seek God.

Ps. 68, iii—"But I am wretched and in pain; may thy help, O God, protect me."

---

34. For the Lord hears the poor, * and despises not his captives.

35. Let heaven and earth praise him, * the seas and whatever stirs therein.

36. For God will save Sion, and rebuild the cities of Juda: * and they shall dwell there and possess it.

37. And the descendants of his servants shall inherit it; * and they who love his name, shall dwell therein.

Glory be to the Father, and to the Son, and to the Holy Ghost.

As it was in the beginning, is now, and ever shall be, world without end. Amen.

Ps. 97—An appeal to the whole world to praise God.

The Lord, Judge and Ruler of the Universe

PSALM 97

Lauds

SING to the Lord a new song, * because he has done wonderful things.

His right hand and his holy arm * have brought him victory.

2. The Lord has made known his salvation, * in the sight of the nations he has revealed his justice.

3. He has been mindful of his goodness and faithfulness * toward the house of Israel.

All the ends of the earth have seen * the salvation of our God.

4. Acclaim the Lord, all the earth, * be glad, rejoice and sing praises.

5. Sing praises to the Lord with the lyre, * with the lyre and the sound of melody,

6. With trumpets and the sound of the horn: * shout joyfully before the king, the Lord.

7. Let the sea roar and the fulness thereof, * the world and those who dwell therein.

8. Let the rivers clap their hands, * let the mountains sing in chorus,

9. Before the Lord, for he comes, * for he comes to rule the earth.

He will rule the world with justice * and the peoples with equity.

Short-lived Man Implores the Eternal God

PSALM 89

O LORD, thou hast been our refuge * throughout the ages.

2. Before the mountains were brought forth, and the earth and the world were born, * even from eternity to eternity thou art, O God.

3. Thou commandest men to return to dust, * and sayest: "Return, O children of men."

4. For a thousand years in thy sight are as yesterday which is past, * and as a watch in the night.

Ps. 89—"The sum of our years is seventy . . . and most of them are toil and trouble: for they quickly pass, and we vanish."

---

5. Thou snatchest them away: they become like a dream in the morning, * like grass that shoots up:

6. In the morning it flourishes and is green, * in the evening it is mowed down and withers.

7. Truly, we are consumed by thy anger, * and terrified by thy indignation.

8. Thou hast set our faults before thee, * our secret sins in the light of thy countenance.

9. For all our days have passed away in thy anger; * we have ended our years like a sigh.

10. The sum of our years is seventy * and, if we are strong, eighty;

And most of them are toil and trouble: * for they quickly pass, and we vanish.

11. Who has considered the power of thy anger, * and thy indignation with the fear that is due to thee?
12. Teach us to number our days, * that we may attain wisdom of heart.
13. Reconsider, O Lord, is it for a long time? * be gracious to thy servants.
14. Fill us quickly with thy kindness, * that we may rejoice and be glad all our days.
15. Gladden us for the days wherein thou hast afflicted us, * for the years wherein we have seen misfortune.
16. Let thy work be manifest to thy servants, * and thy glory to their children.
17. And may the goodness of the Lord, our God be upon us, and the work of our hands do thou prosper for us, * and the work of our hands do thou prosper.

The Marvels of Divine Grace

PSALM 35

SIN speaks to the wicked man in his heart; * there is no fear of God before his eyes.
3. For in his mind he flatters himself * that his fault will not be found out and hated.
4. The words of his mouth are iniquity and deceit, * he has ceased to be wise and to do good.

5. He plans iniquity upon his bed, * he determines on a course that is not good, he does not turn in horror from evil.

6. O Lord, thy mercy reaches to heaven, * thy faithfulness to the very clouds.

7. Thy justice is as the mountains of God, thy judgments are as the deep sea: * thou savest men and beasts, O Lord.

8. How precious is thy goodness, O God: * men take refuge under the shadow of thy wings;

9. They are satiated with the abundance of thy house, * and thou givest them to drink of the torrent of thy delights.

10. For with thee is the fountain of life, * and in thy light we see light.

11. Continue thy goodness to those who worship thee, * and thy equity to the upright of heart.

12. Let not the foot of the proud come upon me, * nor the hand of the sinner drive me out.

13. Behold, the evildoers have fallen: * they are overthrown and can rise no more.

Jeremias, the Prophet

Canticle of Jeremias

(JER. 31, 10-14)

HEAR the word of the Lord, you nations, * and declare it in the islands that are afar off,

And say: he who scattered Israel, will gather him, * and will guard him as a shepherd does his flock.

11. For the Lord will redeem Jacob, * and will deliver him from the hand of one mightier than he.

12. And they shall come, and sing on Mount Sion, * and they shall flock together for the good things of the Lord,

For the corn and wine and oil, * and for the young of the cattle and of the herds.

And their soul shall be as a watered garden, * and they shall faint no more.

13. Then shall the virgin rejoice in the dance, * and young men and old men together.

And I will turn their mourning into joy, * and I will console and make them joyful after their sorrow.

14. And I will refresh the soul of the priests with fat offerings, * and my people shall be filled with my good things.

Praise the Lord: the Provider of His People

PSALM 146

PRAISE the Lord, for he is good, * sing praises to our God, for he is gracious: praise befits him.

2. The Lord rebuilds Jerusalem, * he gathers together the dispersed of Israel;

3. He heals the broken-hearted, * and binds up their wounds.

4. He determines the number of the stars, * he calls each one by name.

5. Great is our Lord and mighty in his strength, * there is no limit to his wisdom.

6. The Lord lifts up the lowly; * the wicked he casts to the ground.

Ps. 146—"Sing to the Lord with thanksgiving . . . who covers the heavens with clouds, who prepares rain for the earth."

---

7. Sing to the Lord with thanksgiving, * sing praises to our God on the lyre.

8. Who covers the heavens with clouds, * who prepares rain for the earth;

Who makes grass to grow on the mountains, * and plants for the service of man;

9. Who gives to the cattle their food, * to the young ravens that cry to him.

10. He delights not in the strength of the horse, * nor does he take pleasure in the fleetness of man.

11. The Lord's delight is in them who fear him, * who put their trust in his goodness.

Ps. 22—"The Lord is my shepherd."

The Good Shepherd

PSALM 22

Prime

THE Lord is my shepherd: I want for nothing;
* he makes me rest in green pastures.
He leads me to waters where I may rest; *
3. he revives my spirit.
He guides me along the right paths * for his name's sake.
4. Even though I walk in a dark valley, * I will fear no evil, for thou art with me.
Thy rod and thy staff: * these comfort me.
5. Thou settest a table for me * in the sight of my enemies;
Thou anointest my head with oil; * my cup overflows.
6. Goodness and kindness shall follow me * all the days of my life,

And I shall dwell in the house of the Lord * for a long time.

The Blessings of Christ's Reign

PSALM 71, I

O GOD, give thy judgment to the king, * and thy justice to the king's son:

2. May he rule thy people with justice, * and thy poor with equity.

3. May the mountains bring peace to the people * and the hills justice.

4. He shall protect the lowly among the people, he shall save the children of the poor, * and shall crush the oppressor. *

5. And he shall live as long as the sun, * and as the moon throughout all ages.

6. He shall descend like rain upon the grass, * like showers that water the earth.

7. In his days justice shall flourish, * and fullness of peace, till the moon be no more.

PSALM 71, II

AND he shall rule from sea to sea, * and from the river to the ends of the earth.

9. His foes shall bow down before him, * and his enemies shall lick the dust.

Man's prayer to the King of Peace

---

10. The kings of Tharsis and of the islands shall offer tribute; * the kings of the Arabians and of Saba shall bring gifts.

11. And all the kings shall worship him, * all nations shall serve him.

12. For he shall deliver the needy one, when he cries, * and the poor man, who has no helper.

13. He shall take pity on the needy and the poor, * and save the life of the poor.

14. He shall redeem them from harm and oppression, * and precious shall be their blood in his sight.

15. Therefore, he shall live, and they shall give him of the gold of Arabia, * and they shall pray for him constantly: they shall bless him perpetually.

Ps. 71, ii—"And all the kings shall worship him, all nations shall serve him."

---

16. There shall be abundance of grain in the land; on the mountain-tops its fruit shall rustle like Lebanon, * and the people of the cities shall flourish like the grass of the field.

17. His name shall be blessed forever; * as long as the sun shines, his name shall endure.

And all the tribes of the earth shall be blessed in him, * all nations shall proclaim him blessed.

18. Blessed be the Lord, the God of Israel, * who alone does wondrous things.

19. And blessed be his glorious name forever; * and may all the earth be filled with his glory. So be it! So be it!

Ps. 72, i—*The just man is tempted to envy the apparent prosperity of the wicked.*

The Apparent Prosperity of the Wicked

PSALM 72, I

Terce

HOW good God is to the upright, * the Lord to those who are clean of heart!

2. Yet my feet almost faltered, * my steps almost slipped,

3. For I envied the wicked, * when I saw the prosperity of the sinners.

4. For they have no torments, * sound and healthy is their body.

5. They are free from the troubles of other men, * and they are not scourged like other men.

6. Therefore pride, like a necklace, encircles them * and violence, like a robe, covers them.

7. Their iniquity proceeds from a gross heart, * the thoughts of their mind break forth.

8. They scoff and speak maliciously, * from on high they threaten oppression.

9. They set their mouths against heaven, * and their tongue reproaches the earth.

A Trial to the Faithful

PSALM 72, II

THEREFORE my people turn to them, * and gulp down great draughts of water.

11. And they say: "How does God know, * and is there knowledge in the Most High?"

12. Behold, such are the wicked * and, always at ease, they increase their wealth.

13. Have I, then, in vain kept my heart clean, * and washed my hands in innocence?

14. For I suffer scourges all the time, * and chastisement daily.

15. Had I thought: I will speak like them, * I should have betrayed the generation of thy children.

16. So I took thought how to understand this; * but it seemed too difficult for me,

17. Until I entered into God's holy counsels, * and considered the end of those wicked men.

Ps. 72, iii—"Whom else have I in heaven but thee? and, if I am with thee, earth does not delight me."

God Alone Our True Happiness

PSALM 72, III

SURELY, thou settest them on a slippery path, * thou dashest them to ruins.

19. How they crashed in an instant, * they vanished, they perished in great terror!

20. As the dream of one awakening, O Lord, * so, on rising, thou wilt spurn their image.

21. When my mind was embittered, * and my heart was vexed,

22. I was senseless and knew nothing: * I was like a dumb animal before thee.

23. Yet I shall always be with thee: * thou takest hold of my right hand;

24. By thy counsel thou wilt guide me, * and at last thou wilt take me into glory.

25. Whom else have I in heaven but thee? * and, if I am with thee, earth does not delight me.

26. My flesh and my heart waste away, * the Rock of my heart and my portion is God forever.

27. For, behold, they who withdraw from thee, shall perish, * thou destroyest all who are unfaithful to thee.

28. But for me, it is good to be near God, * to put my trust in the Lord God.

I will declare all thy works, * within the gates of the daughter of Sion.

Act of Reparation

PSALM 73, I

Sext

WHY, O God, hast thou cast us off forever, * why does thy anger rage against the sheep of thy pasture?

2. Remember thy congregation, which thou didst establish of old, the tribe, which thou didst redeem as thy possession, * Mount Sion, which thou hast made thy dwelling place.

3. Direct thy steps to the irreparable ruins: * the foe has laid waste everything in the sanctuary.

Ps. 73, i—*"The foe has laid waste everything in the sanctuary . . . they are like those who swing the axe in a thicket."*

---

4. Thy foes have roared in the place of thy assembly, * they have set up their emblems as trophies.

5. They are like those who swing the axe in a thicket, * and now with axe and hammer they likewise smash its gates.

7. They have set thy sanctuary on fire, * they have profaned the dwelling place of thy name even to the ground.

8. They said to themselves, "Let us destroy them all at once; * burn all God's sanctuaries in the land."

9. No longer do we see our signs, there is no prophet; * and there is not one among us who knows how long it will last.

Ps. 73, ii—"Thou didst divide the sea by thy might, didst shatter the heads of the dragons in the waters."

Recalling God's Past Favors

PSALM 73, II

HOW long, O God, shall the foe revile? * shall the enemy blaspheme thy name forever?

11. Why dost thou withdraw thy hand * and keep thy right hand within thy bosom?

12. Yet God is my king of old, * who works salvation in the midst of the earth.

13. Thou didst divide the sea by thy might, * didst shatter the heads of the dragons in the waters.

14. Thou didst crush the heads of Leviathan, * thou gavest him as food to the monsters of the sea.

15. Thou didst bring forth fountains and streams: * didst dry up ever flowing rivers.

16. Thine is the day and thine is the night; * thou didst make firm the moon and the sun.

17. Thou hast set all the boundaries of the earth; * summer and winter thou hast fashioned.

Prayer for Help

PSALM 73, III

REMEMBER this: the enemy has reviled thee, O Lord, * and a senseless people has blasphemed thy name.

19. Deliver not to the vulture the life of thy turtledove: * forget not forever the life of thy poor.

20. Look upon thy covenant, * for the dark places of the land and the fields are full of violence.

21. Let not the oppressed be turned back in confusion: * may the poor and the needy praise thy name.

22. Arise, O God, take up thy cause; * remember that the senseless insult thee every day.

23. Forget not the outcry of thy foes: * the uproar of thy enemies rises continually.

Ps. 74,—"There is a cup in the Lord's hand . . . And he pours therefrom . . . all the wicked of the earth shall drink."

Warning of God's Coming Judgment

PSALM 74

None

WE give thanks to thee, O God, we give thanks, * we proclaim thy name, we recount thy wonders.

3. "When I set the time, * I will judge justly.

4. Though the earth be shaken with all its inhabitants: * I have established its pillars.

5. I say to the insolent: 'Be not insolent,' * and to the wicked: 'Do not flaunt your power':

6. Lift not your head against the Most High * speak not arrogantly against God.

7. For there is no help from the East nor from the West, * neither from the desert nor from the mountains:

8. But God is the judge: * he humbles one and exalts another.
9. For there is a cup in the Lord's hand, * with foaming wine, full of spices:
And he pours therefrom; even its dregs they shall drain, * all the wicked of the earth shall drink."
10. But as for me, I will rejoice forever, * I will sing praises to the God of Jacob,
11. And I will break all the powers of the wicked; * the power of the just shall be exalted.

Thanksgiving for Victory over Temptation

PSALM 75, I

GOD is known in Juda, * his name is great in Israel.
3. His tabernacle is in Salem, * and his dwelling in Sion.
4. There he shattered the fiery shafts of the bow, * the shield, the sword, and the weapons of war . . .
5. In a shining light thou, O Mighty One, didst come * from the everlasting hills.
6. The stout-hearted were despoiled; * they are sunk in deep sleep, the hands of all the warriors have failed.
7. At thy rebuke, O God of Jacob, * chariots and horses sank to the ground.

PSALM 75, II

THOU art to be feared, and who can resist thee, * because of the violence of thy wrath?

9. From heaven thou didst pronounce sentence: * the earth feared and was silent,

When God arose in judgment * to save all the humble of earth.

11. For the fierce men of Edom shall praise thee, * and the survivors of Emath shall keep a festival for thee.

12. Make vows to the Lord your God and fulfill them, * let all round about him bring gifts to him who is to be feared,

13. To him who restrains the spirit of princes, * who is awe-inspiring to the kings of the earth.

Ps. 132—"Behold, how good and how pleasant it is, for brethren to dwell together in unity."

Fraternal Charity

PSALM 132

Vespers

BEHOLD, how good and how pleasant it is, * for brethren to dwell together in unity:

Like the precious oil upon the head, that ran down upon the beard, the beard of Aaron, * that ran down to the edge of his robe;

It is as if dew like the dew of Hermon * were falling upon Mount Sion:

For there the Lord bestows blessing, * life forevermore.

Ps. 135, i—The Wonders of Creation.

Praise the Creator!

PSALM 135, I

PRAISE the Lord, for he is good, * for his mercy is everlasting.

2. Praise the God of gods, * for his mercy is everlasting.

3. Praise the Lord of lords, * for his mercy is everlasting.

4. Who alone did great wonders, * for his mercy is everlasting.

5. Who with wisdom made the heavens, * for his mercy is everlasting.

6. Who spread out the earth upon the waters, * for his mercy is everlasting:

7. Who made the great lights, * for his mercy is everlasting:

8. The sun to rule over the day, * for his mercy is everlasting,

9. The moon and the stars to rule over the night, * for his mercy is everlasting.

Praise the Redeemer!

PSALM 135, II

WHO smote the Egyptians in their first-born, * for his mercy is everlasting.

11. Who brought forth Israel from their midst, * for his mercy is everlasting,

12. With a mighty hand and an outstretched arm, * for his mercy is everlasting.

13. Who divided the Red Sea into parts, * for his mercy is everlasting.

14. And he led Israel through the midst of it, * for his mercy is everlasting.

15. And he cast Pharaoh and his army into the Red Sea, * for his mercy is everlasting.

16. Who led his people through the desert, * for his mercy is everlasting.

17. Who struck down great kings, * for his mercy is everlasting.

18. And he slew mighty kings, * for his mercy is everlasting:

Ps. 135, ii—The Providence of God. "Who gives food to all creatures, for his mercy is everlasting."

---

19. Sehon, king of the Amorites, * for his mercy is everlasting,

20. And Og, king of Basan, * for his mercy is everlasting,

21. And he gave their land for a possession, * for his mercy is everlasting,

22. For a possession to Israel, his servant, * for his mercy is everlasting.

23. Who remembered us in our lowliness, * for his mercy is everlasting.

24. And he delivered us from our foes, * for his mercy is everlasting.

25. Who gives food to all creatures, * for his mercy is everlasting.

26. Praise the God of heaven, * for his mercy is everlasting.

Ps. 136—"By the rivers of Babylon, there we sat and wept, when we remembered Sion."

Homesick for Heaven

PSALM 136

BY the rivers of Babylon, there we sat and wept, * when we remembered Sion.

2. On the willows of that land * we hung up our harps.

3. For there, our captors asked songs of us, and our tormentors, mirth: * "Sing us some of the songs of Sion!"

4. How could we sing a song of the Lord * in a foreign land?

5. If I forget thee, O Jerusalem, * may my right hand forget its skill!

6. Let my tongue cleave to my palate, * if I remember thee not,

If I set not Jerusalem * above all my joy.

7. Bear in mind, O Lord, against the children of Edom, * the day of Jerusalem,

Who said: "Destroy, destroy * the very foundations thereof!"

8. O daughter of Babylon, destructive one, * happy he who repays you the evils you have brought upon us!

9. Happy he who shall seize and dash * your little ones against the rock!

Prayers of Thanksgiving

PSALM 137

I WILL give thee thanks, O Lord, with my whole heart, * for thou hast heard the words of my mouth;

In the presence of the angels I will sing

2. praises to thee,' * I will prostrate myself toward thy holy temple,

And I will praise thy name * because of thy kindness and faithfulness,

For thou hast magnified above all * thy name and thy promise.

3. When I called upon thee, thou didst answer me, * thou didst increase strength within me.

4. All the kings of the earth shall give thee thanks, O Lord, * when they hear the words of thy mouth;

Ps. 137—"Indeed the Lord is high, yet he looks upon the lowly."

---

5. And they shall sing of the ways of the Lord: * "Great indeed is the glory of the Lord."

6. Indeed the Lord is high, yet he looks upon the lowly, * but the proud he regards from afar.

7. Though I walk in the midst of tribulation, thou dost preserve my life, thou stretchest forth thy hand against the wrath of my enemies, * thy right hand saves me.

8. The Lord will complete his work in my behalf. O Lord, thy kindness is everlasting; * forsake not the work of thy hands.

Ps. 69—*"I am wretched and poor, O God help me! Thou art my helper and liberator: O Lord do not delay."*

Prayer in Time of Trouble

PSALM 69

Compline

BE pleased, O God, to rescue me; * O Lord, make haste to help me.

3. Let them be put to confusion and shame * who seek my life.

Let them be turned back and humiliated, * who delight in my misfortunes.

4. Let them fall back, covered with confusion, * who say to me: Ha, Ha!

5. Let them rejoice and be glad because of thee, * all who seek thee;

And let them who love thy help say always: "God is great."

6. But I am wretched and poor, * O God, help me!

Thou art my helper and liberator: * O Lord, do not delay.

Prayer for Perseverance

PSALM 70, I

TO thee, O Lord, I flee for refuge: * let me never be put to shame;

2. In thy justice deliver me and rescue me; * incline thy ear to me and save me.
3. Be thou a rock of refuge to me, a fortress to save me: * for thou art my rock and my stronghold.
4. O my God, rescue me from the hand of the sinner, * from the fist of the evildoer and the violent:
5. For thou art my trust, O my God, * O Lord, my hope from my youth.

6. Upon thee have I leaned from birth; from my mother's womb thou wast my protector: * in thee I hoped always.

7. I have appeared as a marvel to many; * for thou wast my strong refuge.

8. My mouth was full of thy praise, * of thy glory all day long.

9. Cast me not off in my old age; * when my strength fails, forsake me not.

Ps. 70, i—"To thee, O Lord, I flee for refuge . . . Be thou a rock of refuge to me."

10. For my enemies talk about me, * and they who watch me take counsel together,

11. Saying: "God has forsaken him; pursue and seize him, * for there is none to deliver him."

12. O God, be not far from me, * O my God hasten to help me.

Past Mercies Inspire Hope for the Future

PSALM 70, II

LET the adversaries of my life be confounded and fail; * let them be covered with confusion and shame who seek my ruin.

14. But I will always hope * and daily contribute to all thy praise.

Ps. 70, ii—*"I also will praise thy faithfulness on the harp, O God, I will sing praise to thee on the lyre, O Holy One of Israel."*

---

15. My mouth shall tell of thy justice, of thy help all the day long: * for I know not their number.

16. I will tell of the might of God, * O Lord, I will proclaim thy justice, thine alone.

17. O God, thou hast taught me from my youth, * and until now I declare thy wonders.

18. And even to old age and gray hairs, * O God, forsake me not,

Till I declare thy strength to this generation, * thy power to all who are to come,

19. And thy justice, O God, which reaches to heaven, * by which thou hast done such great things: O God, who is like to thee?

20. Thou hast laid many, grievous trials upon me: * thou wilt restore me again and raise me again from the depths of the earth.

21. Increase my honor, * and again comfort me.

22. I also will praise thy faithfulness on the harp, O God, * I will sing praise to thee on the lyre, O Holy One of Israel.

23. My lips shall rejoice, when I sing praises to thee, * and my soul, which thou hast redeemed.

24. My tongue also shall speak of thy justice all day long, * because they who seek my ruin are disgraced and covered with shame.

Glory be to the Father, and to the Son, and to the Holy Ghost.

As it was in the beginning, is now, and ever shall be, world without end. Amen

Ps. 77, i—"He set up a precept . . . and established a law."

Remember and Repent

I Nocturn **PSALM 77, I** Matins

HEARKEN, my people, to my teaching; * incline your ears to the words of my mouth.

2. I will open my mouth in parables, * I will reveal the secrets of past ages.

3. What we have heard and known, * and what our fathers have told us,

4. We will not hide from their children, * to the coming generation we will declare The praises of the Lord and his might * and the wonders he has wrought.

5. For he set up a precept in Jacob * and established a law in Israel,

Which he commanded our fathers, * to make known to their children,

6. That the coming generation, children yet unborn, * should know that they should rise and tell their children,

7. To put their hope in God and not forget the works of God, * but to keep his commandments;

8. Lest they become, like their fathers, * a rebellious and stubborn generation:

A generation with an inconstant heart, * with a spirit unfaithful to God.

God's Goodness

PSALM 77, II

THE children of Ephraim fighting with the bow * turned back in the day of battle.

10. They kept not the covenant of God, * and refused to follow his law,

11. And they forgot his deeds, * and his wonders which he had shown them.

12. In the sight of their fathers he performed miracles * in the land of Egypt, in the field of Tanis.

13. He divided the sea and led them through, * he made the waters stand like a rampart.

Ps. 77, ii—"He brought forth streams from the rock."

---

14. He led them by a cloud during the day, * with a fiery light all through the night.

15. He split rocks in the wilderness, * and gave them drink in abundance as out of the deep sea.

16. He brought forth streams from the rock, * and made waters flow like rivers.

Man's Ingratitude

PSALM 77, III

BUT they continued to sin against him, * to offend the Most High in the desert.

18. And they tempted God in their hearts, * by demanding food according to their craving.

Ps. 77, iii—"And he rained flesh upon them like dust, and winged birds like the sand of the sea."

---

19. And they spoke against God; * they said: "Can God spread a table in the wilderness?

20. Behold, he struck the rock, so that water gushed out and streams poured forth: * can he also give bread, or furnish meat to his people?"

21. Therefore, when the Lord heard, he became angry, and fire was kindled against Jacob, * and wrath blazed against Israel,

22. For they believed not God, * nor trusted in his help.

23. Yet he commanded the clouds above, * and he opened the gates of heaven,

24. And he rained manna upon them for food, * and heavenly bread he gave them.

25. Man ate the bread of the strong: * he sent them provisions in abundance.

26. He raised the east wind in the heavens * and by his power guided the south wind.

27. And he rained flesh upon them like dust, * and winged birds like the sand of the sea.

28. And these fell in the midst of their camp, * round about their tents.

29. So they ate and were well filled, * and he satisfied their desire.

30. They had not yet left off their craving, and their food was still in their mouth, *

31. when the wrath of God blazed against them,

And he slew their princes, * and laid low the youth of Israel.

Sin, Punishment, Pity

PSALM 77, IV

II Nocturn

YET they sinned still more, * and believed not in his miracles.

33. Therefore, he ended their days quickly, * and their years in sudden ruin.

34. When he was slaying them, they sought him, * they returned and inquired of God;

Ps. 77, iv—The brazen serpent. "Yet he, in his mercy, forgave their guilt, and did not destroy them."

---

35. And they remembered that God was their rock, * and the Most High God their redeemer.

36. But they deceived him with their mouth, * and lied to him with their tongue.

37. And their heart was not steadfast toward him, * nor were they loyal to his covenant.

38. Yet he, in his mercy, forgave their guilt, and did not destroy them, and often he checked his anger, * and did not pour out all his wrath.

39. And he remembered that they were but flesh, * a breath that passes and does not return.

Ps. 77, v—*The angel of death over Egypt.*

Israel's Sins; God's Miracles

PSALM 77, V

HOW often they provoked him in the desert, * and grieved him in the wilderness!

41. And still again they tempted God, * and vexed the Holy One of Israel.

42. They remembered not his power, * the day when he delivered them from the oppressor,

43. When he wrought his signs in Egypt, * and his wonders in the field of Tanis,

44. And when he turned their rivers to blood * and their streams, so that they could not drink.

45. He sent among them flies which devoured them, * and frogs which molested them;

46. He gave up their crops to the grasshopper, * and the fruit of their labor to the locust.

47. He destroyed their vines with hail, * and their sycamore trees with frost.

48. He exposed their cattle to the hail, * and their flocks to the lightnings.

49. He sent against them his fierce anger, wrath and fury and affliction: * an embassy of messengers of woe.

50. He opened a way for his wrath: he spared them not from death, * and delivered their animals to the plague.

51. And he struck every first-born in Egypt, * the first-fruits of their manhood in the tents of Cham.

52. And he led forth his people like sheep, * and guided them like a flock in the desert.

53. And he led them on safely, so that they were not afraid, * and the sea overwhelmed their enemies.

54. And he brought them to his holy land, * to the mountains which his right hand had won;

55. He drove out the nations before them, and by lot he apportioned their possession, * and settled the tribes of Israel in their tents.

Ps. 77, vi—"And he chose David, his servant, and took him from the sheepfolds."

God's Punishment

PSALM 77, VI

BUT they tempted and provoked God, the Most High, * and kept not his precepts.

57. They turned back and were faithless like their fathers, * and they wandered from the way like a treacherous bow.

58. They angered him with their shrines in high places, * and aroused his jealousy with their graven images.

59. God heard and became exceedingly angry, * and violently rejected Israel.

60. He forsook the sanctuary of Silo, * the tabernacle where he dwelt among men.

61. And he surrendered its strength into captivity, * and its glory into the hands of the foe.

62. And he delivered his people to the sword, * and raged against his inheritance.

63. Fire devoured their young men, * and their virgins were not betrothed.

64. Their priests fell by the sword, * and their widows did not mourn.

65. Then the Lord awoke as from a sleep * like a warrior overcome by wine.

66. And he struck his foes from behind: * he inflicted upon them a lasting disgrace.

67. And he rejected the house of Joseph, * and chose not the tribe of Ephraim.

68. But he chose the tribe of Juda, Mount Sion which he loved.

69. And he built his sanctuary high as heaven, * *firm* as the earth, which he founded forever.

70. And he chose David, his servant, * and took him from the sheepfolds:

71. From the care of ewes he called him to shepherd Jacob, his people, * and Israel, his inheritance.

72. He shepherded them with an upright heart, * and led them with skilful hands.

Ps. 78—"They have given the corpses of thy servants as food to the birds of the air."

Desecration and Lamentation

PSALM 78 III Nocturn

O GOD, the nations have come into thy inheritance, they have defiled thy holy temple, * they have reduced Jerusalem to ruins.

2. They have given the corpses of thy servants as food to the birds of the air, * the flesh of thy faithful to the beasts of the earth.

3. They have poured out their blood like water all round Jerusalem, * and there was none to bury them.

4. We have become a reproach to our neighbors, * an object of derision and mockery to those around us.

5. How long, O Lord? wilt thou be angry forever? * will thy jealousy burn like fire?

6. Pour out thy wrath on the nations that know thee not, * and upon the kingdoms that invoke not thy name.

7. For they have devoured Jacob, * and laid waste his dwelling place.

8. Do not hold against us the guilt of our forefathers; let thy mercy quickly come to us: * for we are exceedingly miserable.

9. Help us, O God of our salvation, because of the glory of thy name, * and rescue us and forgive our sins for thy name's sake.

10. Why should the heathen say: * "Where is their God?"

Let the vengeance for thy servants' blood which has been shed * be made known among the heathens before our eyes.

11. May the moaning of the prisoners reach thee; * by thy great power release those who are doomed to death.

12. And pay back to our neighbors sevenfold into their bosom * the outrage which they have heaped on thee, O Lord.

13. But we, thy people, and the sheep of thy pasture, will honor thee forever; * throughout all ages we will declare thy praise.

Ps. 80—"Thou shalt not have a strange god, nor shalt thou worship any foreign god: I am the Lord, thy God."

Celebrate God's Feasts Worthily

PSALM 80

SING aloud to God our helper, * acclaim the God of Jacob.

3. Intone the hymn and sound the tamborine, * the sweet-sounding harp with the lyre.

4. Blow the trumpet at the new moon, * at the full moon, on our solemn feast,

5. For it is a statute of Israel, * an ordinance of the God of Jacob.

6. He made it a law in Joseph, * when he went forth against the land of Egypt.

I heard words which I had never before

7. understood:' "I freed his shoulder from the burden; * his hands were freed from the load-basket.

8. In trouble thou didst call and I rescued thee; I answered thee out of the thundercloud, * I tested thee by the waters of Meriba.

9. Hear, O my people, I will admonish thee: * Israel, if thou wouldst but listen to me!

10. Thou shalt not have a strange god, * nor shalt thou worship any foreign god:

11. I am the Lord, thy God, who brought thee out of Egypt: * open wide thy mouth, and I will fill it.

12. But my people did not listen to my voice, * and Israel did not obey me.

13. So I abandoned them to the hardness of their heart: * let them follow their own devices.

14. Oh, that my people would listen to me, * that Israel would walk in my ways:

15. I would at once subdue their enemies, * and turn my hand against their foes;

16. Those who hate the Lord would fawn upon him, * and their lot would last forever.

17. But I would feed *Israel* with the best of wheat, * and with honey from the rock would I satiate them."

Ps. 82—*"My God, make them like leaves in a whirlwind, like chaff before the wind."*

A Cry for Help against Enemies

PSALM 82

O LORD, be not silent; * hold not thy peace, O God, be not still.

3. For, behold, thy enemies are in an uproar, * and they who hate thee lift up their head.

4. Against thy people they devise schemes, * and plot against those protected by thee.

5. They say: "Come let us destroy them as a nation, * that the name of Israel be remembered no more."

6. Truly, with one mind they conspire, * and against thee they make an alliance:

7. The tents of Edom and the Ismaelites, * Moab and the Agarenes,

8. Gebal, Ammon and Amalec, * Philistia with the people of Tyre;

9. The Assyrians too are their allies, * they lend their strength to the children of Lot.

10. Deal with them as with Madian, * as with Sisara and Jabin by the brook Cison,

11. Who were destroyed at Endor, * they became as dung for the ground.

12. Make their chiefs like Oreb and Zeb, * all their princes like Zebee and Salmana,

13. Who said: * "Let us seize for ourselves the regions of God."

14. My God, make them like leaves in a whirlwind, * like chaff before the wind.

15. As fire burning up a forest, * and as a flame setting the mountains ablaze,

16. So pursue them with thy storm, * with thy tempest dismay them.

17. Fill their faces with shame, * that they may seek thy name, O Lord.

18. Let them be put to shame and terrified forever, * let them be disgraced and perish.

19. And let them know that thou, whose name is the Lord, * alone art the Most High over the whole earth.

Ps. 98—*"In a pillar of cloud he spoke to them: they heard his commandments and the precept which he gave them."*

Holy God, We Praise Thy Name

PSALM 98

Lauds

THE Lord is king: the peoples tremble; * he sits above the Cherubim: the earth quakes.

2. The Lord is great in Sion * and high above all the peoples.

3. Let them praise thy great and awe-inspiring name: * it is holy.

4. And he is king, the mighty one, who loves justice: thou hast established what is right, * justice and right thou dost exercise in Jacob.

5. Exalt the Lord, our God, and prostrate yourselves at his footstool: * it is holy.

6. Moses and Aaron are among his priests, and Samuel among those who called upon his name: * they called upon the Lord, and he answered them.

7. In a pillar of cloud he spoke to them: * they heard his commandments, and the precept which he gave them.

8. O Lord, our God, thou didst answer them; O God, thou wast gracious to them, * but thou didst punish their wrong-doing.

9. Exalt the Lord, our God, and prostrate yourselves at his holy mountain: * for holy is the Lord, our God.

A Penitential Prayer

PSALM 142

O LORD, hear my prayer, listen to my entreaty according to thy faithfulness, * answer me according to thy justice.

2. Bring not thy servant to trial, * for in thy sight no man living is just.

3. For the enemy pursues me: he has crushed my life to the earth, * he has made me to dwell in darkness like those long dead.

4. And my spirit faints within me; * my heart within me grows numb.

Ps. 142—"The enemy pursues me: he has crushed my life to the earth, he has made me to dwell in darkness like those long dead."

5. I recall the days of old, I meditate on all thy deeds, * I consider the works of thy hands.

6. I stretch out my hands to thee; * my soul thirsts for thee like parched land.

7. Hasten to answer me, O Lord: * for my spirit fails.

Hide not thy face from me, * lest I become like those who go down into the pit.

8. Let me experience thy mercy speedily, * for I trust in thee.

Show me the way in which I should walk, * for to thee I lift up my soul.

9. Deliver me from my enemies, O Lord: * in thee I hope.

10. Teach me to do thy will, * for thou art my God.

Thy spirit is good: * may it guide me on level ground.

11. For thy name's sake, O Lord, save my life; * in thy mercy bring me out of distress.

12. And in thy kindness cut off my enemies, and bring to naught all who afflict me: * for I am thy servant.

The Blessing of Absolution

PSALM 84

THOU hast favored thy land, O Lord; * thou hast restored the fortunes of Jacob.

3. Thou hast forgiven the guilt of thy people; * thou hast pardoned all their sins.

4. Thou hast withdrawn all thy anger, * thou hast turned away the fury of thy wrath.

5. Restore us, O God, our Savior, * and abandon thy wrath against us.

6. Wilt thou be angry with us forever, * or prolong thy anger for all times?

7. Wilt thou not again revive us, * and will not thy people rejoice in thee?

8. Show us, O Lord, thy mercy, * and grant us thy salvation.

Ps. 84—*The return of the exiles. "Restore us, O God, our Savior, and abandon thy wrath against us."*

---

9. I will listen to what the Lord God will say: * truly he speaks of peace

To his people, to his faithful, * and to those who turn their hearts to him.

10. Surely his salvation is near to those who fear him, * that glory may dwell in our land.

11. Mercy and faithfulness shall unite, * justice and peace shall embrace.

12. Faithfulness shall spring from the earth, * and justice shall look down from heaven.

13. The Lord will also give prosperity, * and our land shall yield its produce.

14. Justice shall go before him, * and salvation in his footsteps.

The Prophet, Isaias.

Canticle of Isaias, 45, 15-26

TRULY thou art a hidden God, * the God of Israel, Savior.

16. All his adversaries * have been disgraced and filled with shame.

Filled with shame * the makers of idols departed.

17. Israel was saved by the Lord with an eternal salvation; * you shall not be disgraced nor be ashamed forever and ever.

18. For so says the Lord, the creator of heaven, * God himself, who formed the earth and made it and established it.

He did not create it to be empty, he formed it to be inhabited: * "I am the Lord, and there is no other.

19. I have not spoken in secret, * in a dark place of the earth;

I have not said to the offspring of Jacob: 'In vain shall you seek me'; * I am the Lord, promising just things, foretelling right things.

20. Assemble, and come, and draw near all of you, * who have been saved from the heathen.

They are foolish, who carry their graven images of wood, * and pray to a god who cannot save.

21. Tell and pour forth the words, consult together: * who has announced this from olden times, who has long since foretold it? Is it not, I, the Lord? and there is no god beside me; * outside of me there is no just and saving god.

22. Turn to me that you may be saved, all ends of the earth: * for I am God, and there is no other.

23. I swear by my very self, truth goes forth from my mouth, * a word that cannot be recalled.

Every knee shall bend to me, * every tongue shall swear.

24. In the Lord only, they shall say of me, is justice and power, * they shall come to him in confusion all who have resisted him.

25. In the Lord all the offspring of Israel shall obtain their right and shall be glorified."

Ps. 147—"Praise thy God, O Sion, for he has strengthened the bars of thy gates."

Thank God for His Blessings

PSALM 147

PRAISE the Lord, O Jerusalem, * praise thy God, O Sion,

13. For he has strengthened the bars of thy gates, * he has blessed thy children within thee.

14. He has established peace on thy borders, * he fills thee with the finest of wheat.

15. He sends out his command to the earth, * his word runs swiftly.

16. He gives snow like wool, * he strews hoarfrost like ashes.

17. He casts down his ice like crumbs of bread; * in the presence of his cold the waters freeze.

18. He sends forth his word and melts them; * he bids his wind to blow and the waters flow.

19. He has declared his word to Jacob, * his statutes and precepts to Israel.

20. He has not done so to any other nation : * his precepts he has not made known to them.

A Prophecy of the Passion

PSALM 21, I

Prime

MY God, my God, why hast thou forsaken me? * thou art far from the prayers, from the words of my cry.

3. My God, I cry during the day, and thou dost not answer, * and in the night, and thou dost not heed me.

4. But thou dwellest in the holy place, * the praise of Israel.

5. In thee our fathers trusted, * they hoped and thou didst deliver them;

6. To thee they cried and they were saved, * in thee they trusted and were not put to shame.

Ps. 21 i—"My God, my God, why hast thou forsaken me?"

---

7. But I am a worm and not a man, * the scorn of men and despised of the people,

8. All who see me scoff at me, * they open wide their mouths and wag their head:

9. "He trusts in the Lord: let him deliver him, * let him save him, if he loves him."

10. Indeed thou didst bring me forth from the womb; * thou madest me secure on my mother's breast.

11. To thee I was committed at my birth, * from my mother's womb thou art my God.

12. Stand not far from me, for I am in distress; draw near: * for there is none to help.

Ps. 21, ii—"They have pierced my hands and my feet."

PSALM 21, II

MANY bullocks are round about me, * the bulls of Basan surround me.
14. They open their mouths against me, * like a ravenous and roaring lion.
15. I am poured out like water, * and all my bones are disjointed:
My heart has become like wax, * melting away within my breast.
16. My throat is dried up like a potsherd, my tongue cleaves to my jaws, * and in the dust of death thou hast laid me.
17. For many dogs surround me, * a gang of evildoers encircles me.
They have pierced my hands and my
18. feet, * I can count all my bones. They indeed look and gloat over me; they

19. divide my garments among them, * and for my vesture they cast lots.

20. But thou, O Lord, stand not far from me: * O my strength, hasten to help me.

21. Rescue me from the sword, * and my life from the power of the dog;

22. Save me from the lion's mouth, * my wretched self from the horns of the buffalo.

The Triumph of the Messias

PSALM 21, III

I WILL declare thy name to my brethren, * in the midst of the assembly I will praise thee.

24. "You who fear the Lord, praise him; all descendants of Jacob, glorify him: * fear him, all descendants of Israel.

25. For he has not spurned nor disdained the suffering of the afflicted; neither did he hide his face from him * and, when he cried to him, he heard him."

26. Thou art the theme of my praise in the great assembly, * my vows will I pay in the sight of those who fear him.

27. The poor shall eat and be satisfied, they who seek the Lord shall praise him: * "May your hearts live forever."

Ps. 21, iii—The triumph of Christ, the Messias.

28. All the ends of the earth * shall remember and turn to the Lord;

And all the families of the nations * shall worship before him,

29. For the kingdom is the Lord's, * and he rules the nations.

30. All who slumber in the earth will worship him alone, * all who go down into the dust will bow before him.

31. But my soul shall live for him, * my descendants shall serve him,

32. I will speak of the Lord to the coming generation, * and they shall declare his justice to a people, yet to be born: "These things has the Lord done."

Ps. 79, i—"Thou hast fed them with the bread of tears and given them tears to drink in abundance."

An Appeal to the Good Shepherd

PSALM 79, I

Terce

SHEPHERD of Israel, give ear, * thou who leadest Joseph like a flock.

Thou, enthroned above the Cherubim,

3. shine forth * before Ephraim, Benjamin and Manasses.

Stir thy might, * and come, to save us.

4. Restore us, O God, * look with favor, that we may be saved.

5. O God of hosts, how long wilt thou be enraged, * in spite of thy people's prayer?

6. Thou hast fed them with the bread of tears * and given them tears to drink in abundance.

7. Thou hast made us an object of strife to our neighbors, * and our enemies mock us.

8. O God of hosts, restore us, * look with favor, that we may be saved.

Restore God's Vineyard

PSALM 79, II

THOU didst take a vine out of Egypt, * thou didst drive out the nations and plant it.

10. Thou didst clear the ground for it, * it took root and filled the land.

11. The mountains were covered with its shadow, * and the cedars of God with its branches.

12. It sent forth its boughs to the sea, * and its shoots to the river.

13. Why hast thou broken down its fence, * so that all who pass by the way strip it,

14. The boar of the forest lays it waste, * and the beasts of the field graze on it?

15. O God of hosts, return, * look from heaven and see, and visit this vine.

16. And protect what thy right hand has planted, * and the shoot which thou hast strengthened for thyself.

17. May they who destroyed it by fire and uprooted it, * perish at the rebuke of thy countenance.

Ps. 79, ii—The spirit of a people weeps over the ravaged vine (Israel). "Why hast thou broken down its fence, so that all who pass by the way strip it."

18. Let thy power be upon the man of thy right hand, * upon the son of man whom thou hast strengthened for thyself.

19. Then we shall not depart from thee anymore; * thou wilt revive us, and we will proclaim thy name.

20. O Lord, God of hosts, restore us, * and look with favor, that we may be saved.

Woe to You, Unjust Judges!

PSALM 81

GOD arises in the divine assembly, * in the midst of the gods he passes sentence.

2. "How long will you judge unjustly, * and favor the cause of the wicked?

3. Uphold the weak and the orphan, * treat justly the lowly and the poor.

4. Rescue the weak and the needy: * deliver them from the power of the wicked."

5. They have neither knowledge nor understanding, they go about in darkness: * all the foundations of the earth are shaken.

6. I said "You are gods, * and sons of the Most High, all of you.

7. Yet you shall die like men, * and fall like any prince."

8. Arise, O God, judge the earth, * for all nations are thy rightful possession.

Prayer for Holy Communion

PSALM 83, I

Sext

HOW lovely is thy dwelling place O, Lord of hosts! * my soul yearns, it

3. pines for the courts of the Lord;
My heart and my flesh * acclaim the living God.

4. Even the sparrow finds a home, * and the swallow a nest for herself, wherein to place her young:
Thy altars, O Lord of hosts, * my king and my God!

5. Happy are they who dwell in thy house, O Lord, * they praise thee without ceasing.

Ps. 83, i—*"Happy are they who dwell in thy house, O Lord."*

---

6. Happy the man whose help is from thee, * when his mind is set on pilgrimage:

7. Passing through the arid valley, they make it a region of springs, * and the early rain clothes it with blessings.

8. They become stronger as they go; * they will see the God of gods in Sion.

PSALM 83, II

LORD of hosts, hear my prayer; * give ear, O God of Jacob.

10. Behold, O God, our shield, * and look upon the face of thy anointed.

11. Truly, one day in thy courts is better * than a thousand others;

Ps. 83, ii—"Truly, one day in thy courts is better than a thousand others."

I had rather stand at the threshold of the house of my God, * than to dwell in the tents of sinners.

12. For the Lord God is a sun and a shield: * the Lord bountifully bestows grace and glory,

He withholds no good thing * from those who walk blamelessly.

13. O Lord of hosts, * happy the man who trusts in thee.

The Church of Christ, the Mother of All

PSALM 86

THE Lord loves his foundation upon the holy mountains: * the gates of Sion more than all the other dwellings of Jacob.

Ps. 86—The City of God.

---

3. Glorious things are said of thee, * O city of God!

4. I will reckon Rahab and Babel among my worshippers: * behold Philistia and Tyre and the people of Ethiopia: these were born there.

5. And it shall be said of Sion: "One and all, they were born therein * and the Most High himself has established it."

6. The Lord will record in the book of the nations: * "These were born there"

7. And they shall sing as they dance: * "All my springs are in thee."

Ps. 88, i—"O Lord, God of hosts, who is like thee? mighty art thou, O Lord."

God's Promises, an Anchor of Hope

PSALM 88, I

None

I WILL sing of the kindness of the Lord forever; * with my mouth I will make known thy faithfulness through all the ages.

3. For thou hast said: "Kindness is set up forever;" * in the heavens thou hast established thy faithfulness.

4. "I have made a covenant with my elect; * I have sworn to David, my servant:

5. I will settle thy offspring forever, * and I will establish thy throne throughout the ages."

6. The heavens praise thy wonders, O Lord, * and thy faithfulness in the assembly of the holy.

7. For who among the clouds can be compared to the Lord, * who is like unto the Lord among the sons of God?
8. God is awe-inspiring in the assembly of the holy, * great and to be feared above all around him.
9. O Lord, God of hosts, who is like thee? * mighty art thou, O Lord, and thy faithfulness surrounds thee.
10. Thou rulest the pride of the sea, * thou stillest the surging of the sea.
11. Thou didst pierce and crush Rahab, * with thy mighty arm thou didst scatter thy enemies.
12. Thine are the heavens, and thine is the earth; * the world and its fulness thou hast founded;
13. The north and the south thou hast created; * Thabor and Hermon rejoice at thy name.
14. Thine is a mighty arm, * strong is thy hand, uplifted thy right hand.
15. Justice and right are the foundation of thy throne; * grace and faithfulness go before thee.
16. Happy are the people who know how to rejoice; * they walk, O Lord, in the light of thy countenance,
17. In thy name they rejoice always, * and by thy justice they are exalted.
18. For thou art the splendor of their strength, * and by thy favor is our might exalted.

19. For our shield belongs to the Lord, * and to the Holy One of Israel, our King.

God's Great Promises

PSALM 88, II

OF old, in a vision, thou didst speak to thy faithful and say: * "I have bestowed a crown on a warrior; I have exalted one chosen from the people.

21. I have found David, my servant, * with my holy oil I have anointed him,

22. That my hand may be with him always, * and my arm may strengthen him.

23. No enemy shall deceive him, * nor shall the wicked afflict him.

24. But I will crush his foes before him, * and will strike those who hate him.

25. My faithfulness and my kindness shall be with him; * and in my name shall his power be exalted.

26. I will set his hand upon the sea, * his right hand upon the rivers.

Ps. 88, ii—"I have bestowed a crown on a warrior; I have exalted one chosen from the people. I have found David, my servant."

---

27. He shall call to me: 'Thou art my Father, * my God and the rock of my salvation.'
28. And I will make him the first-born, * the highest of all kings on earth.
29. Forever will I continue my kindness to him, * and my covenant shall stand firm with him.
30. I will make his offspring to endure forever, * his throne as the days of heaven.
31. If his sons forsake my law, * and walk not in my ordinances,
32. If they profane my statutes, * and do not keep my commandments:
33. I will punish their offense with the rod * and their guilt with stripes;
34. But I will not take away my kindness from him, * nor will I be false to my pledged word.

35. I will not violate my convenant, * nor change the utterance of my lips.

36. Once have I sworn by my holiness: * I will certainly not lie to David,

37. His descendants shall continue forever * and his throne shall be as the sun before me,

38. Like the moon, established forever, * a faithful witness in heaven.

A Prayer for Help

PSALM 88, III

BUT thou hast cast off and rejected, * thou art very angry with thy anointed.

40. Thou hast spurned the covenant with thy servant, * and hast defiled his crown in the dust.

41. Thou hast broken down all his walls, * his strongholds thou hast laid in ruin.

42. All who pass by the way plunder him, * he has become a laughing-stock to his neighbors.

43. Thou hast exalted the right hand of his foes, * and gladdened all his enemies.

Ps. 88 iii—"Thou hast broken down all his walls . . . How long, O Lord? wilt thou hide thyself forever?"

---

44. Thou hast blunted the edge of his sword, * and hast not upheld him in battle.

45. Thou hast put an end to his splendor, * and hurled his throne to the ground.

46. Thou hast shortened the days of his youth, * and covered him with shame.

47. How long, O Lord? wilt thou hide thyself forever? * shall thy wrath burn like a fire?

48. Remember how short my life is, * how frail thou hast made all men.

49. What man shall live and not see death, * and deliver his soul from the power of the abyss?

50. Where are thy former kindnesses, O Lord, * which thou didst pledge to David by thy faithfulness?

51. Remember, O Lord, the disgrace of thy servants: * I bear in my bosom all the enmities of the nations,

52. Wherewith thy enemies revile, O Lord, * wherewith they revile the footsteps of thy anointed.

53. Blessed be the Lord forever: * So be it! So be it!

God Knows All, Sees All

PSALM 138, I

Vespers

O LORD, thou searchest and knowest me, * thou knowest me, when I sit down and when I stand up.

Thou discernest my thoughts from afar;

3. thou seest me walking and lying down, * and thou art familiar with all my ways.

4. A word is not yet on my tongue: * behold, O Lord, thou knowest it all beforehand.

5. Behind and before thou dost encompass me, * and thou layest thy hand upon me.

6. Such knowledge is too wonderful for me, * sublime: far beyond me.

Ps. 138, i—*The All-knowing God.*

---

7. Whither can I go from thy spirit? * whither can I flee from thy presence?

8. If I ascend into heaven, thou art there; * if I am prostrate in the abyss, thou art there.

9. If I take up the wings of the dawn, * if I dwell at the end of the sea:

10. Even there thy hand will guide me, * and thy right hand hold me fast.

11. If I say: "At least darkness shall cover me, * and night like light surround me:"

12. Darkness itself is not dark to thee, and night shines as the day: * to thee darkness is as light.

Ps. 138, ii—"Examine me, O God, and know my heart; . . . and see, whether I walk a crooked way, and do thou lead me."

God is All-powerful

PSALM 138, II

FOR thou didst create my inner being, * thou didst fashion me in my mother's womb.

14. I praise thee, that I was made so wonderfully, * that thy works are marvelous.

And my soul thou knowest full well, *

15. my frame was not hidden from thee, When I was fashioned in secret, * and put together in the depths of the earth.

16. Thy eyes beheld my deeds, and all were written in thy book; * days were decreed, while yet there was not one of them.

17. How difficult for me are thy designs, O God, * how vast the sum of them!

18. Were I to count them, they are more than the sands; * were I to come to the end of them, I would still be with thee.

19. Oh, that thou wouldst slay the wicked, O God, * and that bloodthirsty men would depart from me!

20. For they rebel against thee with evil intent, * treacherously thy enemies rise up against thee.

21. Do I not hate those who hate thee, O Lord, * do I not loathe those who rise up against thee?

22. With perfect hatred I hate them; * they are my own enemies.

23. Examine me, O God, and know my heart; * try me, and know my sentiments,

24. And see, whether I walk a crooked way,* and do thou lead me in the way of old.

Prayer for Protection against Lying Lips

PSALM 139

DELIVER me, O Lord, from the evil man, * from the violent man preserve me:

3. From those who devise evil in their heart, * who daily stir up strife,

Ps. 139—"Keep me, O Lord, from the hands of the wicked."

---

4. They sharpen their tongue like a serpent: * under their lips is the venom of adders.

5. Keep me, O Lord, from the hands of the wicked, * from the violent man preserve me:

6. Who plan to trip my steps, * the proud have hidden a snare for me,

And spread cords as a net, * by the wayside they set traps for me.

7. I say to the Lord: Thou art my God; * hearken, O Lord, to the voice of my supplication.

8. O Lord, God, my mighty help ! * thou shieldest my head on the day of battle.

9. Grant not, O Lord, the desires of the wicked man, * do not fulfill his plans.

10. Those who surround me lift up their head: * let the malice of their lips overwhelm them.

11. Let him rain burning coals upon them; * let him cast them into the pit, never to rise.

12. A man of evil tongue shall have no standing in the land; * evil shall entrap the violent man suddenly.

13. I know that the Lord will render right to the needy, * justice to the poor.

14. Surely the just shall give praise to thy name, * the upright shall dwell in thy presence.

Lead Us not into Temptation!

PSALM 140

O LORD, I call to thee: hasten to help me; * listen to my voice, when I call to thee.

2. Let my prayer rise to thee like incense, * the lifting up of my hands like the evening sacrifice.

3. Set a guard, O Lord, over my mouth, * keep watch at the door of my lips.

4. Incline not my heart to any evil, * to engage in wicked deeds;

And with men who do wrong * let me never feed on their choice foods.

Ps. 140—"Let my prayer rise to thee like incense, the lifting up of my hands like the evening sacrifice."

---

5. Let the just man strike me: it is kindness; * let him rebuke me: it is oil for the head,

Which my head shall not refuse, * but I will always pray under their corrections.

6. Beside the rock their leaders were let go free, and they heard, * how mild my words were.

7. As when the plowman breaks a furrow in the ground, * so their bones lie scattered at the entrance to the abyss.

8. For to thee, O Lord God, my eyes are turned; * in thee I take refuge: take not away my life.

9. Keep me from the trap they have set for me, * and from the snares of evildoers.

10. May the wicked fall together into their own nets, * while I pass on safely.

The Prayer of a Soul in Great Distress

PSALM 141

I CRY aloud to the Lord, * aloud I beseech the Lord.

3. I pour out my complaint before him, * and my distress I lay before him.

4. When my spirit grows faint within me, * thou knowest my path.

In the way in which I walk, * they have hidden a snare for me.

5. I look to the right and see, * there is no one to befriend me.

There is no escape for me, * no one who cares for my life.

6. I cry to thee, O Lord, I say: Thou art my refuge, * my portion in the land of the living.

7. Give heed to my cry, * I have become very wretched.

Deliver me from my pursuers, * for they are stronger than I am.

8. Bring me out of prison, * that I may give thanks to thy name.

The just shall surround me, * when thou dealest kindly with me.

Ps. 76, i—*"In the day of my distress I seek the Lord."*

Meditation on the Ways of God

PSALM 76, I

Compline

MY voice rises to God and I cry, my voice rises to God that he may hear

3. me; * in the day of my distress I seek the Lord.

By night my hand is outstretched unweariedly; * my soul refuses to be comforted.

4. When I recall God, I moan; * when I meditate, my spirit grows faint.

5. Thou holdest open my eyes; * I am troubled and cannot speak.

6. I ponder upon the days of old, * and I recall the years long past.

7. I muse in my heart by night, * I meditate and my spirit inquires:

8. "Will God cast *us* off forever, * will he never again be gracious?

9. Will his kindness cease forever, * will his promise come to nought throughout all ages?

10. Has God forgotten to show mercy? * has he in anger shut up his compassion?"

11. Then I say: "This is my grief, * that the right hand of the Most High has changed."

12. I recall the deeds of the Lord, * surely, I recall thy wonders of old.

13. I meditate on all thy works, * and I ponder upon thy deeds.

The Ways of God are Wonderful

PSALM 76, II

O GOD, thy way is holy: * what god is as great as our God?

15. Thou art the God who workest wonders, * thou hast made known thy power among the peoples.

16. With thy arm thou hast redeemed thy people, * the sons of Jacob and Joseph.

Ps. 76, ii—"The crash of thy thunder came in a whirlwind, lightnings lit up the world: the earth quaked and trembled."

17. The waters saw thee, O God, the waters saw thee: they trembled, * and the depths quaked.

18. The clouds poured forth waters, the skies sent forth a sound, * and thy arrows flew around.

19. The crash of thy thunder came in a whirlwind, lightnings lit up the world: * the earth quaked and trembled.

20. Thy way led through the sea, and thy path through the great waters, * but thy tracks could not be seen.

21. Thou didst lead thy people like a flock, * by the hand of Moses and Aaron.

Ps. 85—"O Lord . . . look upon me and be gracious to me . . . give me a sign of thy favor that they who hate me, may see and be put to shame."

Deliver Us from Evil

PSALM 85

INCLINE thy ear, O Lord, answer me, * for I am needy and poor.

2. Preserve my life, for I am devoted to thee; * save thy servant who trusts in thee.

3. Thou art my God: be gracious to me, O Lord, * for I cry to thee constantly.

4. Gladden the soul of thy servant, * for to thee, O Lord, I lift up my soul.

5. For thou, O Lord, art good and forgiving, * rich in mercy towards all who call upon thee.

6. Hearken, O Lord, to my prayer, * and heed the voice of my supplication.

7. In the day of my trouble I call upon thee, * for thou wilt answer me.

8. There is none like thee among the gods, O Lord, * and there are no works like thine:

9. All the nations, which thou hast made, shall come and worship thee, O Lord, * and they shall glorify thy name.

10. For thou art great and workest wonders: * thou alone art God.

11. Teach me, O Lord, thy way, that I may walk in thy truth; * direct my heart, that it may fear thy name.

12. I will thank thee, O Lord, my God, with all my heart, * and I will glorify thy name forever,

13. For thy mercy toward me has been great, * and thou hast delivered my soul from the depths of hell.

14. O God, insolent men have risen up against me, and a crowd of powerful men seek my life, * and they do not set thee before their eyes.

15. But thou, O Lord, art a God merciful and gracious, * slow to anger, exceedingly kind and faithful.

16. Look upon me and be gracious to me; * give thy strength to thy servant, and save the son of thy handmaid.

17. Give me a sign of thy favor, that they, who hate me, may see and be put to shame, * because thou, O Lord, hast helped me and comforted me.

Glory be to the Father, and to the Son, and to the Holy Ghost.
As it was in the beginning, is now, and ever shall be, world without end. Amen.

Ps. 104, i—Abraham sights the Promised Land.

God's Providence in History

I Nocturn **PSALM 104, I** Matins

GIVE thanks to the Lord, proclaim his name, * make known his deeds among the nations.

2. Sing to him, make melody to him, * relate all his wondrous deeds.

3. Glory in his holy name; * let the heart of those who seek the Lord rejoice.

4. Consider the Lord and his power, * seek his face continually.

5. Remember the marvelous deeds he has done, * his wonders, and the judgments of his mouth,

6. Race of Abraham, his servant, * children of Jacob, his elect!

7. He the Lord is our God; * his judgments prevail throughout the world.

8. He remembers his covenant forever, * the promise which he made for a thousand generations,

9. The covenant he made with Abraham, * and the oath he gave to Isaac,

10. Which he established as a statute for Jacob, * and an everlasting covenant for Israel,

11. Saying: To thee will I give the land of Canaan * as your allotted inheritance.

12. When they were few in number, * very few and strangers in that land,

13. When they wandered from nation to nation, * from one kingdom to another people,

14. He permitted no one to oppress them, * and for their sake he rebuked kings:

15. "Touch not my anointed ones, * and do my prophets no harm."

God's Care of His Chosen Ones

PSALM 104, II

THEN he called a famine upon the land; * and took away all means of sustenance.

Ps. 104, ii—Aaron's rod is changed into a serpent. "Then he sent Moses, his servant, and Aaron whom he had chosen. They wrought his signs among them."

---

17. He sent a man before them; * Joseph was sold as a slave.

18. They bound his feet with fetters, * his neck was put into an iron band,

19. Until his prediction came to pass, * until the word of the Lord confirmed him.

20. The king sent and released him, * the very ruler of the peoples, and set him free.

21. He made him lord of his house, * and ruler of all his possessions,

22. That he might instruct his princes as he pleased * and teach his elders wisdom.

23. Then Israel came to Egypt, * and Jacob sojourned in the land of Cham.

24. He increased his people greatly, * and made them stronger than their foes.

25. He turned their heart to hate his people, * to deal treacherously with his servant:

26. Then he sent Moses, his servant, * and Aaron whom he had chosen.

27. They wrought his signs among them, * and wonders in the land of Cham.

God Punishes His Enemies and Liberates His People

PSALM 104, III

HE sent darkness, and it became dark, * but they resisted his words.

29. He turned their waters into blood, * and killed their fish.

30. Their land swarmed with frogs, * even to the chambers of their kings.

31. He spoke and there came a swarm of flies, * and gnats into all their borders.

32. He gave them hail for rain, * flaming fire throughout their land.

33. He struck down their vines and their fig trees, * and shattered the trees within their borders.

34. He spoke, and locusts came, * grasshoppers without number;

Ps. 104, iii—"And he led forth his people with joy, his elect with gladness."

---

35. And they devoured all the plants in their land, * and devoured the fruits of their soil.

36. And he struck all the first-born in their land, * the first-fruits of all their strength.

37. And he led them forth with silver and gold, * and there was no weakling in their tribes.

38. Egypt rejoiced at their going, * for fear *of Israel* had fallen upon them.

39. He spread out a cloud as a screen, * and fire to give light by night.

40. They asked, and he brought quails, * and he satisfied them with bread from heaven.

41. He split the rock, and water gushed forth, * it flowed in the desert like a river.

42. For he remembered his sacred promise, * which he had given to Abraham, his servant.

43. And he led forth his people with joy, * his elect with gladness.

44. And he gave them the lands of the nations, * and they took possession of the riches of the people,

45. That they might keep his statutes, * and obey his laws.

The Mercy of God, the Ingratitude of Man

PSALM 105, I

II Nocturn

GIVE thanks to the Lord, for he is good, * for his kindness is everlasting.

2. Who can recount the mighty deeds of the Lord, * or proclaim all his praises?

3. Happy are they who observe the precepts, * who practise justice at all times!

4. Remember me, O Lord, when thou showest favor to thy people; * visit me with thy help,

5. That I may take delight in the happiness of thy elect, that I may rejoice in the joy of thy people, * that I may glory with thy inheritance.

6. We have sinned as did our fathers, * we have done wrong, we have acted wickedly.

Ps. 105, i—"The waters covered their foes: not one of them was left."

---

7. Our fathers in Egypt * disregarded thy wonders, They remembered not the abundance of thy mercies, * but rebelled against the Most High at the Red Sea.

8. Yet he saved them for his name's sake, * to make known his power.

9. And he rebuked the Red Sea and it was dried up, * and he led them through the waves as through a desert.

10. And he saved them from hostile hands, * and delivered them from the hand of the enemy.

11. But the waters covered their foes: * not one of them was left.

12. Then they believed his words, * and sang his praises.

13. They soon forgot his deeds: * they trusted not his counsel.

14. They gave themselves up to lust in the wilderness, * and tried God in the desert.

15. And he granted them their request, * but sent a plague among them.

16. They envied Moses in the camp, * Aaron, the holy one of the Lord.

17. The earth opened and swallowed up Dathan, * and covered the clan of Abiron.

18. And fire broke out in their clan: * a flame consumed the wicked.

False Worship

PSALM 105, II

THEY made a calf at Horeb, * and adored the idol of molten gold.

20. And they exchanged their glory * for the image of a bullock that eats grass.

21. They forgot God, who had saved them, * who had done great deeds in Egypt,

22. Marvels in the land of Cham, * wonders at the Red Sea.

23. So he was minded to destroy them, * had not Moses, his elect,

Pleaded with him, * to turn back his wrath from destroying them.

Ps. 105, ii—"They made a calf at Horeb and adored the idol of molten gold."

---

24. Then they scorned the desirable land; * they believed not his word.

25. And they murmured in their tents, * they obeyed not the Lord.

26. Therefore with uplifted hand he swore to them, * that he would overthrow them in the desert,

27. And scatter their descendants among the nations, * and disperse them through the lands.

28. And they clung to Beelphegor, * and ate the sacrifices of lifeless idols.

29. They provoked him by their crimes, * and a plague broke out among them.

30. But Phinees stood up and executed judgment, * and the plague ceased.

31. And it was credited to his merit, * throughout the ages forever.

32. Then they angered him at the waters of Meriba, * and it went ill with Moses on their account,

33. For they embittered his spirit, * and he spoke rashly with his lips.

Punishment and Restoration

PSALM 105, III

THEY did not destroy the heathen, * as the Lord had commanded them.

35. But they mingled with the heathen, * and imitated their practices;

36. And they worshipped their idols, * and these became a snare to them.

37. And they sacrificed their sons * and their daughters to demons.

38. And they shed innocent blood: the blood of their sons and of their daughters, * whom they sacrificed to the idols of Canaan.

39. And the land was polluted with blood, and they were defiled by their deeds * and they became unfaithful by their crimes.

40. Therefore, the wrath of the Lord was kindled against his people, * and he abhorred his inheritance.

41 And delivered them into the hands of the nations, * and they who hated them ruled over them.

42. And their enemies oppressed them, * and they were humbled under their hand.

43. Many times he delivered them; but they embittered him by their counsels, * and were brought low because of their iniquities.

44. Yet he looked upon their affliction, * when he heard their cry.

45. And for their sake he remembered his covenant, * and relented according to his abundant mercy.

46. And he made them objects of compassion, * with all who had taken them captive.

47. Save us, O Lord, our God, * and gather us from among the nations.

That we may praise thy holy name, * and glory in thy praise.

48. Blessed be the Lord, the God of Israel, from age unto age: * and let all people say: Amen! Alleluia!

Ps. 106, i—"And they cried to the Lord in their distress, and he delivered them from their troubles."

Gratitude for Redemption

PSALM 106, I

III Nocturn

GIVE thanks to the Lord, for he is good, * for his mercy is everlasting.

2. So let the redeemed of the Lord speak, * whom he has redeemed from the hand of the enemy,

3. And gathered from the lands, from the east and the west, * from the north and the south.

4. They wandered in the wilderness, in the desert, * they found no way to an inhabited town.

5. They were hungry and thirsty, * their strength was failing within them.

6. And they cried to the Lord in their distress; * and he delivered them from their troubles.

7. And he led them by a straight way, * that they might come to an inhabited town.

8. Let them give thanks to the Lord for his mercy, * and for his wondrous deeds toward men.

9. For he has satisfied the starving soul, * and filled the hungry soul with good things.

10. They sat in darkness and in gloom, * prisoners in want and chains.

11. Because they rebelled against the words of God, * and they spurned the counsel of the Most High.

12. So he humbled their hearts with troubles, * they stumbled and there was no one to help.

13. And they cried to the Lord in their distress; * and he delivered them from their troubles.

14. And he brought them out of darkness and gloom, * and broke their bonds.

15. Let them give thanks to the Lord for his mercy, * and for his wondrous deeds toward men,

16. For he has broken the bronze gates * and burst the iron bars.

Ps. 106, ii—*"They who had gone down to the sea in ships, . . . saw the works of the Lord, and his marvels on the sea. At his word a stormy wind arose, that tossed on high the waves of the sea."*

Acts of Divine Mercy

PSALM 106, II

THEY were sick because of their iniquity, * and were afflicted because of their crimes;

18. They loathed every kind of food, * and they came near the gates of death.

19. They cried to the Lord in their distress; * and he delivered them from their troubles.

20. He sent forth his word to heal them, * and to rescue them from destruction.

21. Let them give thanks to the Lord for his mercy, * and for bis wondrous deeds toward men.

22. And let them offer sacrifices of thanksgiving * and declare his works with joy.

23. They who had gone down to the sea in ships, * to trade on the mighty waters,

24. They saw the works of the Lord, * and his marvels on the sea.

25 At his word a stormy wind arose, * that tossed on high the waves of the sea.

26. They mounted up to the heavens, they sank to the depths; * their courage weakened in their plight.

27. They reeled and staggered like drunken men; * and all their skill was gone.

28. And they cried to the Lord in their distress; * and he brought them out of their troubles.

29. He stilled the storm to a gentle breeze, * and the waves of the sea were hushed.

30. And they rejoiced, because they were calmed, * and he led them to their desired haven.

31. Let them give thanks to the Lord for his mercy, * and for his wondrous deeds toward men.

32. Let them thank him in the assembly of the people, * and praise him in the gathering of the elders.

Ps. 106, iii—"And they sowed fields and planted vineyards, which yielded abundant crops."

The Wonderful Providence of God

PSALM 106, III

HE turned rivers into a desert, * and springs of water into parched ground,

34. A fruitful land into a salt waste, * because of the wickedness of those who dwelt therein.

35. He turned a desert into a pool of water, * and an arid land into springs of water.

36. And there he settled the hungry, * and they founded a city to dwell in.

37. And they sowed fields and planted vineyards, * which yielded abundant crops.

38. And he blessed them, so that they multiplied exceedingly, * and he granted them cattle in abundance.

39. Yet they decreased and were brought low * through the pressure of adversity and sorrow;

40. But he, who pours contempt upon princes * and makes them wander in a pathless waste,

41. Raised the needy out of misery * and made families numerous as flocks.

42. The upright see and rejoice, * and all wickedness closes its mouth.

43. Whoever is wise, let him observe these things, * and weigh well the mercies of the Lord.

Hymn of Triumph

PSALM 149

Lauds

SING to the Lord a new song; * let his praise resound in the assembly of the faithful.

2. Let Israel rejoice in her maker, * let the children of Sion exult in their king.

3. Let them praise his name in the dance, * with timbrel and harp let them make music to him,

Ps. 149—"For the Lord loves his people, and he adorns the lowly with victory."

---

4. For the Lord loves his people, * and he adorns the lowly with victory.

5. Let the faithful rejoice in glory, * let them be glad on their couches.

6. Let the praises of God be in their mouth, * and two-edged swords in their hands:

7. To execute vengeance on the nations, * punishments on the peoples;

8. To bind their kings with chains, * and their nobles with iron fetters;

9. To execute upon them the appointed judgment: * this is an honor for all his faithful.

Ps. 91—*"The just man shall flourish like the palm tree, like the cedar of Lebanon he shall grow."*

Praise God, the Just Judge!

PSALM 91

IT is good to give thanks to the Lord, * and to sing to thy name, O Most High:

3. To declare thy goodness in the morning * and thy faithfulness during the hours of the night

4. On the ten-stringed instrument and the lyre, * with a song on the harp.

5. For thou makest me glad, O Lord, by thy deeds, * I rejoice in the works of thy hands.

6. How great are thy works, O Lord, * how exceedingly deep thy thoughts!

7. The senseless man knows not, * nor does the fool know this.

8. Even if the wicked flourish like grass, * and all evildoers prosper,

9. They are doomed to eternal ruin: * but thou art exalted forever, O Lord.

10. For, behold, thy enemies, O Lord, for, behold, thy enemies shall perish: * all evildoers shall be scattered.

11. Thou hast given me strength like that of the buffalo; * thou hast anointed me with the purest oil.

12. And my eye has looked down upon my enemies, * and my ears have heard glad tidings of the wicked who rise up against me.

13. The just man shall flourish like the palm tree, * like the cedar of Lebanon he shall grow.

14. Planted in the house of the Lord, * in the courts of our God they shall flourish.

15. They shall bear fruit even in old age, * fresh and green shall they be,

16. That they may declare, that the Lord is righteous, my Rock, * in whom there is no wrong.

Ps. 63—*"Protect me from the council of the wicked . . . who aim their poisoned words like arrows, to shoot from ambush at the innocent."*

A Prayer for Protection against Enemies

PSALM 63

HEAR my voice, O God, when I complain; * preserve my life from the terror of the foe.

3. Protect me from the council of the wicked * from the tumult of evildoers,

4. Who whet their tongues like a sword, * who aim their poisoned words like arrows,

5. To shoot from ambush at the innocent, * to shoot at him suddenly and unafraid.

6. They firmly set their heart on evil, they plan how to lay their snares secretly, * they say: "Who will see them?"

7. They devise wicked deeds, they hide well-planned schemes, * and the mind and heart of each one is deep.
8. But God strikes them with arrows, * they are suddenly pierced with wounds,
9. And their own tongue brings about their fall: * all who see them shake their heads.
10. And all men see and declare the work of God, * and ponder his deeds.
11. The just man rejoices in the Lord and takes refuge in him, * and all the upright of heart give him glory.

Canticle of Ecclesiasticus

ECCLESIASTICUS 36, 1-16

HAVE pity on us, God of the universe, and look upon us, * and inspire all
2. the nations with a fear of thee.
3. Lift up thy hand against foreign nations, * that they may recognize thy power.
4. As in their sight thou didst show thyself holy among us, * so in our sight show thyself glorious among them,
5. That they may know, just as we know, * that there is no god beside thee, O Lord.
6. Renew the signs and repeat the won-
7. ders; * glorify thy hand and thy right arm.
8. Stir up anger and pour forth fury; *

"Have pity on us, God of the universe."

---

9. remove the foe and destroy the enemy.

10. Hasten the time and decide the end, * that they may declare thy great works.

11. Let him who tries to escape be devoured by a flame of wrath, * and let them who afflict thy people be destroyed.

12. Crush the heads of the enemies' rulers, * who say: "There is none but ourselves."

13. Gather all the tribes of Jacob, * and grant them an inheritance as in the days of old.

14. Have pity, O Lord, on thy people who bear thy name, * and on Israel whom thou hast named the first-born.

15. Have pity on thy holy city, Jerusalem, * the place of thy dwelling.

16. Fill Sion with thy praises, * and thy temple with thy glory.

Ps. 150—Praise the Lord in his sanctuary . . . Praise him with the blast of the horn, praise him with harp and lyre.

Let All Creation Praise God

PSALM 150

PRAISE the Lord in his sanctuary, * praise him in his majestic firmament.

2. Praise him for his mighty deeds, * praise him for his supreme majesty.

3. Praise him with the blast of the horn, * praise him with harp and lyre.

4. Praise him with timbrel and dance, * praise him with strings and pipe.

5. Praise him with loud-sounding cymbals, praise him with crashing cymbals: * let every being that breathes praise the Lord !

Ps. 93, i—"How long shall the wicked glory, . . . They trample on thy people, O Lord, . . . They slay the widow and the stranger, and they murder the orphans."

An Appeal to the Judge of the World

PSALM 93, I

Prime

O LORD, God of vengeance, * God of vengeance shine forth.

2. Arise, thou judge of the earth; * render to the proud what they deserve.

3. How long shall the wicked, O Lord, * how long shall the wicked glory,

4. Pour forth arrogant talk, * how long shall evildoers brag?

5. They trample on thy people, O Lord, * and they afflict thy inheritance;

6. They slay the widow and the stranger, * and they murder the orphans.

7. They say: The Lord does not see, * nor does the God of Jacob take notice.

8. Understand, you fools among the people, * and you senseless ones, when will you be wise?

9. Shall he who made the ear not hear? * or he who formed the eye not see?

10. Shall he who instructs the nations not reprove? * he who teaches men knowledge?

11. The Lord knows the thoughts of men: * indeed they are vain.

The Triumph of Justice over Injustice

PSALM 93, II

HAPPY the man whom thou dost instruct, O Lord, * and dost teach by thy law,

13. To give him relief from evil days, * until a pit is dug for the wicked.

14. For the Lord will not cast off his people, * nor will he forsake his inheritance;

15. But judgment shall become just again, * and all the upright of heart shall follow it.

16. Who will rise up for me against the wicked? * who will stand up for me against evildoers?

17. Had not the Lord been my helper, * my soul would have soon dwelt in the realm of silence.

Ps. 93, ii—*"Happy the man whom thou dost instruct, O Lord, and dost teach by thy law."*

---

18. When I think: "My foot is slipping," * thy grace, O Lord, upholds me.

19. When cares abound within me, * thy consolations delight my soul.

20. Can the throne of wickedness have fellowship with thee, * which frames mischief under the guise of law?

21. Let them assail the life of the just, * and condemn innocent blood:

22. The Lord will certainly be my stronghold, * my God will be the rock of my refuge.

23. And he will repay them their iniquity, and because of their own wickedness he will destroy them, * the Lord, our God, will destroy them.

Ps. 107—*"My heart is steadfast, O God, my heart is steadfast; I will chant and sing praises. Awake, O my soul, awake, harp and lyre! I will awaken the dawn."*

Trust in God

PSALM 107

MY heart is steadfast, O God, my heart is steadfast; * I will chant and sing praises.

3. Awake, O my soul; awake, harp and lyre! * I will awaken the dawn.

4. I will praise thee, O Lord, among the peoples, * and I will sing praises to thee among the nations,

5. For thy goodness is great, even unto the heavens, * and thy faithfulness unto the clouds.

6. Be thou exalted, O God, above the heavens; * may thy glory be over all the earth.

7. That thy beloved may be delivered, * help with thy right hand, and answer us.

8. God has spoken in his sanctuary: * "I will rejoice and I will divide Sichem, and I will measure out the valley of Succoth;

9. Mine is the land of Galaad, and mine is the land of Manasses, * and Ephraim is the defense of my head, Juda my scepter.

10. Moab is my wash-basin; upon Edom I cast my sandal, * over Philistia I will shout in triumph."

11. Who will bring me into the fortified city? * who will lead me into Edom?

12. Is it not thou, O God, who hast rejected us, * and wilt thou not march forth once again, O God, with our armies?

13. Give us help against the foe, * for man's help is futile.

14. Through God we shall do valiantly, * and he will crush our enemies.

A Penitential Prayer

PSALM 101, I

Terce

LORD, answer my prayer, * and let my cry come to thee.

3. Hide not thy face from me * in the day of my distress.

Ps. 101, i—"My days are like lengthened shadows and I am withering away like grass."

Incline thy ear to me: * when I call thee, answer me speedily.

4. For my days vanish like smoke, * and my bones burn like fire.

5. My heart, scorched like grass, is withering away, * I forget to eat my food.

6. Because of the violence of my moaning, * my bones cleave to my skin.

7. I am like a pelican in the wilderness, * I have become like an owl among ruins.

8. I am sleepless and I moan * like a solitary bird on the housetop.

9. My enemies are always insulting me; * they who rage against me, swear by my name.

10. For I eat ashes like bread, * and mingle my drink with tears,

11. Because of thy indignation and thy wrath, * for thou hast lifted me up and cast me down.

12. My days are like lengthened shadows, * and I am withering away like grass.

God is Faithful to His Promises

PSALM 101, II

BUT thou, O Lord, dost abide forever, * and thy name throughout all ages.

14. Arise and have pity on Sion, * because now is the time for thee to be gracious to it, for the hour has come.

15. For thy servants love its stones, * and they have pity on its ruins.

16. Then the nations will fear thy name, O Lord, * and all the kings of the earth thy glory,

17. When the Lord restores Sion * and appears in his glory,

18. When he regards the prayers of the needy, * and does not reject their prayer.

19. Let this be written for a future generation, * and let a people yet unborn praise the Lord.

Ps. 101, ii—The Wailing Wall. "O Lord, . . . Arise and have pity on Sion . . . For thy servants love its stones, and they have pity on its ruins."

20. For the Lord has looked down from his sanctuary on high, * from heaven he has looked upon the earth,

21. To hear the groans of the captives, * to set free those doomed to death,

22. That the name of the Lord might be proclaimed in Sion, * and his praise in Jerusalem,

23. When the peoples are gathered together * and the kingdoms, to serve the Lord.

PSALM 101, III

HE has worn out my strength in the way, * he has shortened my days.

Ps. 101, iii—*"O my God, take me not away in the midst of my days."*

---

25. I say: O my God, take me not away in the midst of my days; * thy years endure throughout the ages.

26. Of old thou didst found the earth, * and heaven is the work of thy hands.

27. They shall perish, but thou wilt endure, * and all things shall grow old like a garment.

As raiment thou changest them, and they

28. are changed: * but thou art the same, and thy years have no end.

29. The children of thy servants shall dwell securely, * and their offspring shall endure before thee.

Ps. 103, i—Bless the Lord, O my soul! . . . Thou didst found the earth upon its bases: it shall not totter forever and ever. Thou didst cover it with the ocean as with a garment, the waters stood upon the mountains.

Praise of the Creator

PSALM 103, I

Sext

BLESS the Lord, O my soul! * O Lord, my God, thou art very great!

Thou art clothed with majesty and beauty,

2. * robed in light as in a mantle.

Thou hast spread out the heavens like a

3. curtain, * thou has built thy chambers above the waters.

Thou makest the clouds thy chariot, * thou walkest upon the wings of the wind.

4. Thou makest the winds thy messengers, * and the flaming fire thy servants.

5. Thou didst found the earth upon its bases: * it shall not totter forever and ever.

6. Thou didst cover it with the ocean as with a garment, * the waters stood upon the mountains.

7. At thy rebuke they fled, * at the sound of thy thunder they were alarmed.

8. The mountains rose, the valleys sank down * to the place which thou hadst determined for them.

9. Thou hast set a bound, beyond which they may not go, * lest they again cover the earth.

10. Thou commandest springs to flow down into brooks * that run between the mountains,

11. They furnish drink to every beast of the field: * wild asses quench their thirst;

12. Beside them the birds of the air dwell, * among the branches they give forth song.

God's Goodness Manifested in Creation

PSALM 103, II

THOU waterest the mountains from thy chambers, * the earth is filled with the fruit of thy works.

14. Thou makest grass to grow for the cattle * and plants for the service of man, That he may bring forth bread from the

Ps. 103, ii—"Thou waterest the mountains from thy chambers, the earth is filled with the fruit of thy works. Thou makest the grass to grow for the cattle and plants for the service of man."

---

15. earth, * and wine that gladdens his heart;
That he may make his face cheerful with oil, * and that bread may strengthen the heart of man.
16. The trees of the Lord have their fill, * the cedars of Lebanon which he planted.
17. There the birds build their nests; * the fir trees are the home of the stork.
18. The high mountains are for the wild goats, * the rocks are a refuge for the rock-rabbit.
19. Thou hast made the moon to mark the seasons; * the sun knows its setting.
20. When thou makest the darkness and night falls, * therein rove all the beasts of the forest.
21. The young lions roar for their prey, * and seek their food from God.

22. When the sun rises, they withdraw, * and lie down in their dens.

23. Man goes forth to his work * and to his labor until the evening.

May the Lord Rejoice in His Works!

PSALM 103, III

HOW many are thy works, O Lord! * thou hast made them all with wisdom: the earth is full of thy creatures.

25. Behold, the sea great and wide: therein are countless creeping things, * animals small and great.

26. There the ships move along, * the Leviathan, which thou hast made to play therein.

27. All look to thee, * to give them food in due season.

28. When thou givest it to them, they gather it; * when thou openest thy hand, they are filled with good things.

29. When thou hidest thy face, they are troubled; when thou takest away their breath, they perish * and return to their dust.

Ps. 103, iii—"Behold the sea great and wide . . . There the ships move along."

---

30. When thou sendest forth thy spirit, they are created, * and thou renewest the face of the earth.

31. May the glory of the Lord be forever: * may the Lord rejoice in his works,

32. Who looks at the earth, and it trembles; * who touches the mountains, and they smoke.

33. I will sing to the Lord, as long as I live; * I will sing praise to my God as long as I am alive.

34. May my song be pleasing to him: * I will rejoice in the Lord.

35. Let sinners be removed from the earth, and the wicked be no more; * bless the Lord, O my soul!

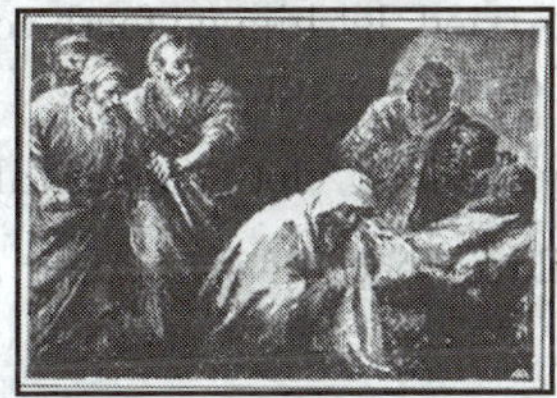

Ps. 108, i—"O God, of my praise, be not silent, for they have opened a wicked and deceitful mouth against me . . . and attacked me without cause."

The Punishments of the Unjust Man

PSALM 108, I

None

O GOD, of my praise, be not silent, * for they have opened a wicked and deceitful mouth against me.

They have spoken to me with a lying

3. tongue,' and surrounded me with words of hatred, * and attacked me without cause.

4. In return for my love they accused me: * but I continued to pray

5. And they have repaid me evil for good, * and hatred for my love.

6. Set thou a wicked man over him, * and let an accuser stand at his right hand.

7. When he is tried, let him go forth condemned, * and let his plea be in vain.

8. Let his days be few, * let another take his office.

9. Let his children become orphans, * and his wife a widow.

10. Let his children become vagrants and beggars, * let them be cast out of their ruined homes.

Woe to the Unmerciful Persecutor

PSALM 108, II

LET the creditor ensnare all his possessions, * and strangers plunder the fruit of his toil.

12. Let there be no one to extend kindness to him, * and let there be no one to pity his fatherless children.

13. Let his offspring be given over to destruction; * in the next generation let their name be blotted out.

14. Let the guilt of his fathers be remembered before the Lord, * and let not his mother's sins be blotted out:

15. Let them be continually before the Lord, * and let him cut off their memory from the earth.

Ps. 108, ii—"Let them be continually before the Lord, and let him cut off their memory from the earth." The woes mentioned in this psalm are a prediction rather than a wish of the psalmist.

16. Because he remembered not to show kindness, but pursued the needy man, the poor, * and the broken-hearted, to kill him.

17. And he loved cursing: may it come upon him; * he loved not blessing: may it be far from him.

18. And let him be clothed with cursing as with a garment: may it go into his being like water, * and, like oil, into his bones.

19. Let it be to him as a garment in which he wraps himself, * and as a cincture with which he is always girded.

Ps. 108, iii—"O Lord, God, . . . deliver me. For I am needy and poor, and my heart is wounded within me."

Prayer for Deliverance

PSALM 108, III

SUCH be the punishment from the Lord, for my accusers, * and for those who speak evil against me.

21. But thou, O Lord, God, act in my behalf for thy name's sake; * because thy mercy abounds, deliver me.

22. For I am needy and poor, * and my heart is wounded within me.

23. I vanish like a lengthening shadow, * and I am shaken off like a locust.

24. My knees tremble because of fasting, * and my flesh is thin and shrunken.

25. And I have become a reproach to them; * when they see me they shake their head.

26. Help me, O Lord, my God; * save me according to thy goodness.

27. And let them know that this is thy hand, * that thou, O Lord, hast done it.

28. Let them curse, but do thou bless; let those who rise up against me be put to shame, * but let thy servant rejoice.

29. Let my accusers be clothed with dishonor, * let them be covered with their shame as with a cloak.

30. I will give thanks to the Lord with my mouth, * and in the midst of the multitude I will praise him:

31. For he has stood at the right hand of the poor man, * to save him from his judges.

Praise of God's Providence

PSALM 143, I

Vespers

BLESSED be the Lord, my Rock, * who trains my hands for battle, my fingers for war,

2. My mercy and my fortress, * my defense and my deliverer,

My shield and my refuge, * who subjects the peoples to me.

Ps. 143, i—"Blessed be the Lord . . . my defense and my deliverer."

---

3. O Lord, what is man that thou dost take care of him, * the son of man that thou thinkest of him?

4. Man is like a breath of air, * his days Like a passing shadow.

5. O Lord, bow thy heavens and come down, * touch the mountains and they shall smoke;

6. Flash forth lightning and scatter them, * send forth thy arrows and rout them;

7. Reach forth thy hand from on high, * rescue me and deliver me out of many waters, from the hand of strangers,

8. Whose mouth speaks falsehood * and whose right hand is raised in perjury.

Ps. 143, ii—"Happy the people whose God is the Lord."

Prophecy of Messianic Blessings

PSALM 143, II

O GOD, I will sing thee a new song, * on a ten-stringed harp I will make music to thee,

10. Who givest victory to kings, * who didst rescue David, thy servant.

11. From the evil sword rescue me, * and deliver me from the hand of strangers, Whose mouth speaks falsehood, * and whose right hand is raised in perjury.

12. May our sons be like plants, * growing up in their youth;

Our daughters like corner pillars, * ornamented like the columns of the temple.

13. May our storehouses be full, * overflowing with all provisions;

May our flocks, a thousandfold fruitful, be increased to myriads in our fields; *

14. may our beasts of burden be well laden.

May there be no breach in our walls, no exile, * no wailing in our streets.

15. Happy the people who fare thus; * happy the people whose God is the Lord.

Praise of God's Great Goodness

PSALM 144, I

I WILL extol thee, my God, O king; * I will bless thy name forever and ever.

2. Every day will I bless thee, * and I will praise thy name forever and ever.

3. Great is the Lord and highly to be praised, * his greatness is unsearchable.

4. One generation praises thy works to another, * and they declare thy might.

5. They tell of the glorious splendor of thy majesty, * and proclaim thy wonders.

6. And they speak of the might of thy tremendous deeds, * and recount thy greatness.

7. They proclaim the praise of thy great goodness, * and rejoice in thy justice.

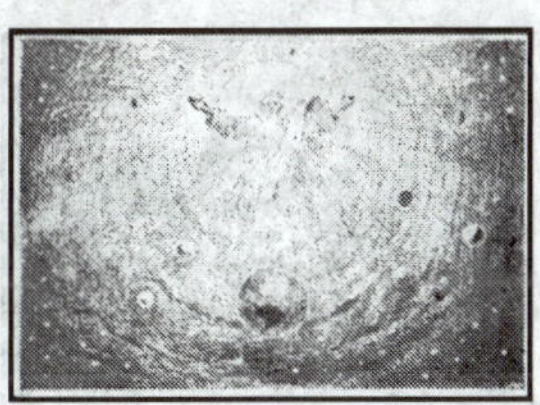

Ps. 144, ii—"The Lord is good to all, and merciful toward all his works."

PSALM 144, II

THE Lord is gracious and merciful, * slow to anger and abounding in kindness.

9. The Lord is good to all, * and merciful toward all his works.

10. Let all thy works praise thee, O Lord, * and let thy faithful bless thee.

11. Let them tell of the glory of thy kingdom, * and proclaim thy might,

12. To make men know thy might, * and the glory of thy magnificent kingdom.

13. Thy kingdom is an everlasting kingdom, * and thy dominion endures throughout all ages.

Ps. 144, iii—*"All eyes turn to thee."*

God will protect His Loyal Worshippers

PSALM 144, III

THE Lord is faithful in all his words, * and holy in all his works.

14. The Lord supports all who fall, * and raises up all who are bowed down.

15. All eyes turn to thee, * and thou givest them food in due season.

16. Thou openest thy hand, * and with benevolence fillest every living thing.

17. Just is the Lord in all his ways, * and holy in all his works.

18. The Lord is near to all who call upon him, * to all who sincerely call upon him.

19. He will fulfill the desire of those who fear him, * he will hear their cry and save them.

20. The Lord guards all who love him, * but all the wicked he will destroy.

21. Let my mouth speak the praise of the Lord, * and let all mortals bless his holy name forever and ever.

Prayer in Time of Desolation

PSALM 87

Compline

LORD, my God, by day I call, * by night I cry out before thee.

3. Let my prayer come before thee, * incline thy ear to my cry.

4. For my soul is full of evils, * and my life is nearing the abyss.

5. I am numbered among those who go down into the pit, * I am like a man without strength.

6. I lie down among the dead, * like the slain who lie in the grave,

Whom thou rememberest no more, * and who are cut off from thy care.

7. Thou hast laid me in a deep pit, * in darkness, in the depths.

8. Thy wrath lies heavy upon me, * and with all thy waves thou dost press down upon me.

Ps, 87—"O Lord . . . let my prayer come before thee . . . I am tike a man without strength. I lie down among the dead, like the slain who lie in the grave."

---

9. Thou hast taken my friends far from me; thou hast made me an utter abomination to them, * I am shut in and cannot go out.

10. My eyes waste away with grief, I cry to thee, O Lord, every day; * I stretch out my hands to thee.

11. Wilt thou work wonders for the dead? * shall the departed arise and praise thee?

12. Shall thy kindness be recounted in the grave, * thy faithfulness in hell?

13. Are thy wonders known in the darkness, * and thy favor in the land of oblivion?

14. But I, O Lord, cry to thee, * and at dawn my prayer comes to thee.

15. Why, O Lord, dost thou reject me, * why dost thou hide thy face from me?

16. I am afflicted and subject to death from my youth, * I have borne thy terrors and become weak.

17. Thy wrath has swept over me, * and thy terrors have overcome me.

18. They surround me like water all day long; * they encircle me completely.

19. Thou hast taken from me friend and comrade: * shadows are my companions.

Praise God for His Mercies!

PSALM 102, I

BLESS the Lord, O my soul, * and let my whole being bless his holy name.

2. Bless the Lord, O my soul, * and forget not all his benefits,

3. Who forgives all your faults, * who heals all your infirmities,

4. Who redeems your life from destruction, * who crowns you with grace and mercy,

5. Who fills your life with good things: * your youth is renewed like the eagle's.

6. The Lord performs works of justice, * and renders justice to all the oppressed.

Ps. 102, i—"Bless the Lord, O my soul, and let my whole being bless his holy name . . . who crowns you with grace and mercy."

---

7. He made known his ways to Moses, * his deeds to the children of Israel.

8. The Lord is merciful and gracious, * slow to anger and abounding in kindness.

9. He will not always contend, * nor will he be angry forever.

10. He does not deal with us according to our sins, * nor repay us according to our faults.

11. For as high as heaven is above the earth, * so great is his goodness toward those who fear him;

12. As far as the east is from the west, * so far has he removed our offenses from us.

Ps. 102, ii—*"Man's days are as grass; like the flower of the field so does he flourish . . . But the goodness of the Lord is forever and ever toward those who fear him."*

God's Mercy is Everlasting

PSALM 102, II

AS a father has compassion on his children, * so the Lord has compassion on those who fear him.

14. For he knows the stuff of which we are made: * he remembers that we are dust.

15. Man's days are as grass; * like the flower of the field so does he flourish:

16. Scarcely does the wind pass over it and it is gone; * and its place knows it no more.

17. But the goodness of the Lord is forever and ever toward those who fear him, * and his justice toward children's children,

18. Toward those who keep his covenant, * and are mindful of his precepts, to observe them.

19. The Lord has established his throne in heaven, * and his sovereignty is supreme.

20. Bless the Lord all his angels, mighty in strength, you who do his bidding, * in order to comply with his command.

21. Bless the Lord, all you his hosts, * his servants, who do his will.

22. Bless the Lord, all you his works, in all the places of his dominion: * bless the Lord, O my soul.

Glory be to the Father, and to the Son,

and to the Holy Ghost.

As it was in the beginning, is now,

and ever shall be, world without end. Amen.

A Call to Praise God

PSALM 94

COME, let us rejoice in the Lord, let us shout with joy to the Rock of our salvation:

2. Let us come into his presence with praises, with songs let us rejoice in him.

3. For the Lord is a mighty God, and a great King above all the gods:

4. In his hand are the depths of the earth, and the tops of the mountains are his.

5. The sea is his: for he made it, and the dry land which his hands formed:

6. Come, let us worship and bow down, let us kneel before the Lord who made us.

7. For he is our God; and we are the people of his pasture and the sheep of his hand.

Would you but listen to his voice today:

8. "Harden not your hearts as in Meriba, as on the day of Massa in the wilderness,

9. Where your fathers tempted me, tried me, although they had seen my works.

10. For forty years I was displeased with that generation, and I said: They are a people with wayward hearts, and they have not recognized my ways.

11. So I swore in my anger: they shall not enter into my rest."

Mary's Gratitude

Canticle of the Blessed Virgin
(Magnificat)

LUKE 1, 46-55

MY SOUL magnifies the Lord;
47. And my spirit rejoices * in God, my Savior,

48. Because he has regarded the lowliness of his handmaid: * for, behold, henceforth all generations shall call me blessed,

49. Because he who is mighty has done great things for me * and holy is his name,

50. And his mercy is from generation to generation * on those who fear him.

51. He has shown might with his arm; * he has scattered the proud in the conceit of their heart.

52. He has put down the mighty from their thrones, * and has exalted the lowly.

53. He has filled the hungry with good things, * and the rich he has sent away empty.

54. He has given help to Israel, his servant, * mindful of his mercy,

55. Even as he spoke to our fathers * to Abraham and to his posterity forever.

The Blessings of Salvation

Canticle of Zachary (Benedictus)

LUKE 1, 68-79

BLESSED be the Lord, the God of Israel, * because he has visited and wrought redemption for his people,

69. And has raised up a horn of salvation for us * in the house of David his servant,

70. As he promised through the mouth of his holy ones, * the prophets from of old:

71. To deliver us from our enemies, * and from the hand of all who hate us,

72. To show mercy to our forefathers * and to be mindful of his holy covenant:

73. Of the oath that he swore to Abraham our father, * that he would grant us,

74. That, delivered from the hand of our enemies * we should serve him without fear,

75. In holiness and justice before him * all our days.

76. And thou, child, shalt be called the prophet of the Most High: * for thou shalt go before the face of the Lord to prepare his ways,

77. To give to his people knowledge of salvation * through forgiveness of their sins

78. Because of the loving-kindness of our God, * wherewith the Orient from on high will visit us,

79. To shine on those who sit in darkness and in the shadow of death, * to guide our feet into the way of peace.

Glory be to the Father, and to the Son,

and to the Holy Ghost.

As it was in the beginning, is now,

and ever shall be, world without end. Amen.

Jesus, the Light of Nations and the Glory of Israel

Canticle of Simeon

LUKE 2, 29-32

NOW thou dost dismiss thy servant, O Lord, * according to thy word in peace,

30. Because my eyes have seen * thy salvation,

31. Which thou hast prepared * before the face of all peoples,

32. A light of revelation to the Gentiles * and the glory of thy people Israel.

Numerical Index

Numerical Index of Psalms

Numerical Index of Psalms

Index

(continued)

MY FAVORITE PSALMS

PSALM NUMBER	PAGE NUMBER

MY FAVORITE PSALMS

PSALM NUMBER	PAGE NUMBER

MY FAVORITE PSALMS

PSALM NUMBER	PAGE NUMBER

MY FAVORITE PSALMS

PSALM NUMBER	PAGE NUMBER